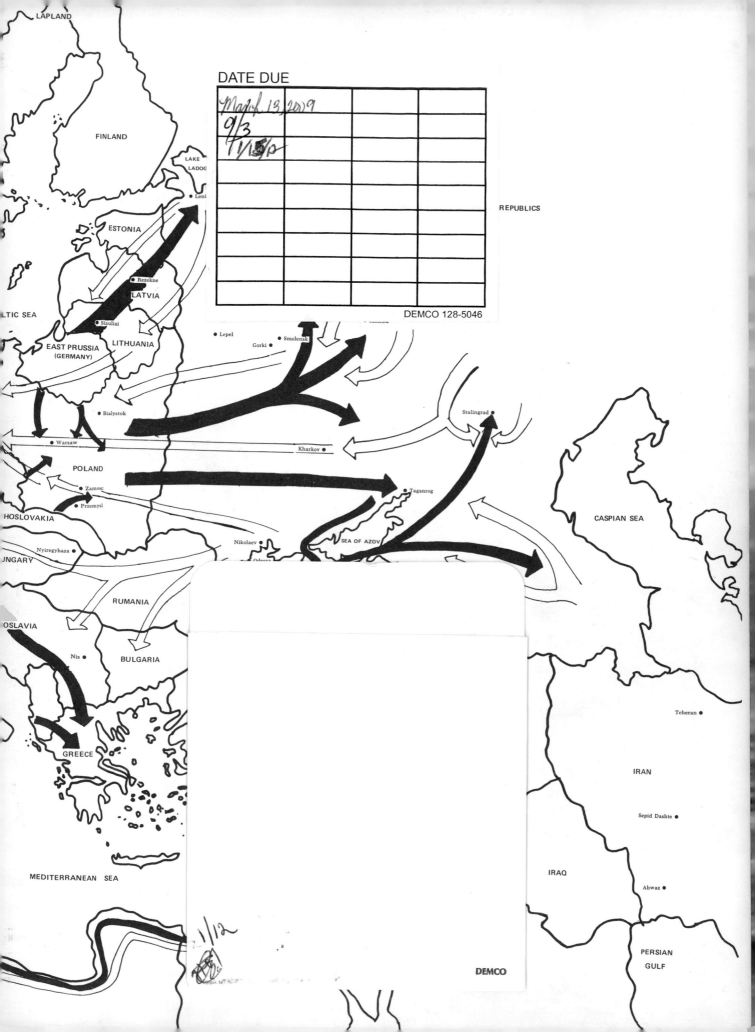

STEEL RAILS
TO VICTORY

Using French equipment, a United States Army hospital train speeds to rear hospitals carrying soldiers wounded on the Rhine front. The date is November 30, 1944, and the River Marne is at flood stage.

U.S. Army

by Ron Ziel
Hawthorn Books, Inc.
Publishers New York

Other Books by Ron Ziel

THE TWILIGHT OF STEAM LOCOMOTIVES
THE STORY OF STEAMTOWN AND EDAVILLE

With George H. Foster:
STEAM IN THE SIXTIES
STEEL RAILS TO THE SUNRISE

With Mike Eagleson:
SOUTHERN STEAM SPECIALS

ACKNOWLEDGMENTS

Individuals, organizations, and government agencies in many of the World War II belligerent powers were of great assistance to the author in gathering the photographs, facts, and anecdotes for this book. Those who devoted the most time in this endeavor include Günter Stetza, of Essen, Germany; Dr. W. Gley, Bundesarchiv, Koblenz; Oberstleutnant Günther Schlötzer, Pionierschule, München; Kolonel Erich Rother, of the German embassy in Washington, D.C.; J. R. Leconte, of the Belgian Royal Army Muscum in Brussels; K. S. Kulkarni, Armed Forces Film and Photo Division, Indian Ministry of Defence, New Delhi; personnel in the various regional offices of the British Railways; Major General W. Thomas Rice, H. W. Martens, and other employees of the Seaboard Coast Line Railroad; President W. Graham Claytor, William F. Geeslin, and C. S. Carbaugh, of the Southern Railway; the public-relations directors and staffs of various other railroads who supplied data and illustrative material; the staffs of government institutions in Washington, including Major Barbara Smith (ret.) and Betty Sprigg, of the Office of the Assistant Secretary of Defense for Public Affairs at the Pentagon; Josephine Motylewski and Paul White, of the National Archives; the staff of the Air Force archives; Lieutenant Chris Dembek, of the 714th Railway Operating Battalion, Fort Eustis, Virginia; and Debbie Allen, of Photoworld in New York. Mrs. Edith Ziel Brandewie, Patricia Cartmell, and Helen A. Smith assisted in the typing of many letters of inquiry. Various translation chores were handled by Yves deKerillis and Carolyn R. Robinson, as well as Mrs. Brandewie. Also assisting in the research were George H. and Helen Foster; James R. Boerckel; James A. Schultz, Vice President, Public Relations, Association of American Railroads; Mike Eagleson and Freeman Hubbard, of *Railroad Magazine*; and Donald P. Kane. A special note of appreciation is expressed to the members of the Military Railway Service Veterans —a dedicated group of gentlemen (amply supported by their ladies) who are keeping alive the memories and traditions of their service as U.S. Army railway men in World War II. Mr. and Mrs. R. E. Godley and the *MRS Journal* did much to put the author in touch with such men as Colonel Fred W. Okie, President of the Bessemer & Lake Erie Railroad; Charles D. ("Doc") Russell; Earl Weed; William T. Church; and many others. No thanks at all to the Ministry of Railways of the USSR, which refused to answer several inquiries, in spite of the assurances of the Russian embassy that the Railway Ministry would be "most cooperative."

STEEL RAILS TO VICTORY

1 2 3 4 5 6 7 8 9 10

Contents

Hitler's Headquarters Car
In 1940, at the height of Adolph Hitler's Career, when he was absolute ruler of Western Europe, he and Foreign Minister Von Ribbentrop disembark from the official headquarters railway car.

Black Star

5

To the memories of two men of God, both of whom spread the Gospel in their own triumphant manner, shared the interest of the author in the railroad legend, and were veritable rocks of spiritual solace during his more melancholy moments, this work is dedicated.

F. NELSON BLOUNT
1918–1967
Railroad Author, Businessman,
Lay Evangelist, Founder of
Steamtown, U.S.A., and Dublin
(N.H.) Christian Academy

REV. FOSTER B. PERRY
1906–1968
Chaplain, Lt. Col., United States
Air Force (ret.), Historian,
Photographer, Minister of the
Bridgehampton Methodist Church

Introduction

Ever since their genesis in the 1820's, railroads and railroad people have played an ever-increasing role in support of tactical maneuvers as well as logistics in wars fought on the land masses of the world. In terms of the sheer magnitude of the tasks performed, the military use of railways in World War II surpassed all previous experience. The individual feats accomplished, as well as the overall importance of the railroads' contributions to the war effort find minimum recognition in the annals of history. This work, with pictorial clarity, pays tribute to the railways and railroaders of World War II and recalls our attention to the undisputed capability of both to strongly influence the balance of power in conflict. To those of us who participated, it also rekindles the nostalgia of this fascinating railroad business, in war as well as in peace. May it also serve as a reminder of the continuing defense needs of all nations for the capability, readiness, and dedication which the railroads and their employees have so ably demonstrated in the past.

W. THOMAS RICE
Major General,
United States Army Reserve
Chairman of the Board,
Seaboard Coast Line Railroad

SCL RR

Major General W. Thomas Rice, United States Army Reserve, was an officer in the Military Railway Service, U.S. Army Transportation Corps, during World War II. He served primarily in the Persian Gulf Service Command, where he was superintendent of the central division of the U.S. Army–operated Iranian State Railway. After the war General Rice went to work for the Richmond, Fredericksburg & Potomac Railroad, and became its president in 1955. As president of the Atlantic Coast Line Railroad since 1957, he was elected president of the Seaboard Coast Line Railroad ten years later, when the ACL merged with the Seaboard Air Line Railroad. He later became Chairman of the Board of Directors. He is also a director of various nationally known companies and organizations, both within and outside the transportation industry. All trains loaded with military supplies bound for Teheran (below) were handled over the division controlled at the time by a young major named W. Thomas Rice.

U.S. Army

Foreword

Even a quarter of a century after the cataclysmic events of World War II passed into the archives of military history, the enormity of the greatest conflict in human existence still numbed the reasoning of its students. There was, of course, the still unanswered question of how the world's most civilized nations could become embroiled in so self-destructive a catastrophe. Probably that question will never be resolved—at least until the reasons for man's nature as a fighting species are finally discovered. The more tangible aspects of the war, however, are most remarkable, and they are the concern of this monograph.

The role played by railways during the Second World War was one of great importance in all theaters of combat and on most of the fronts. From hastily constructed light railways right in forward positions to the vast, efficient rail networks existing in the interior of every belligerent power, all battle plans had to take the railroad situation into serious consideration. The simple facts were that where the rail lines operated unhindered, the vast quantities of war supplies—raw materials for the mills and factories and finished products for the front lines—were delivered on or close to schedule. Where rail service was delayed and finally destroyed, the armies depending on it were greatly compromised and eventually defeated in the field. All the major forces had their railway troops for construction, repair, operation, and defense. When retreating, some even had specialized detachments charged with the demolition of railway facilities. All these elements of wartime railway operations will be reviewed in this volume.

The inherent characteristics of economy and flexibility in railways as a mode of transport were revealed in every phase of the war. As the railroads of entire continents were called to carry as much as double their normal capacity, approximately one third of their employees were drafted into military service. In addition, with the exceptions of North America, Australia, the Middle East, and most of India, these same railroads suffered immense destruction. In the instances of France by mid-1944 and Germany by early 1945, this destruction was virtually total. In spite of these incredible adversities, trains kept rolling, even if they sometimes could no longer effectively support armies which were, for all practical purposes, already defeated.

Because of their many useful combat characteristics, railways were prime targets in all military planning. On the ground the objective of many a major offensive was to secure a certain railhead or a line between vital facilities, with the dual purpose of utilizing such a line for one's own logistics while denying its use to the enemy. Huge artillery guns rode the rails. Antiaircraft guns mounted in formidable batteries on rail cars could be moved from one sector to another, as targets for aerial bombardment shifted. Perhaps the most fascinating aspect of railway operations during this period was the armored trains employed by many of the warring nations—particularly on the eastern front in Europe.

It is significant that the first strategic air raid by the great American bombers which were eventually to play a decisive role in the defeat of the Axis powers was directed against a railway objective: the Sotteville marshaling yards near Rouen, in occupied France. The date was August 17, 1942, and the embryonic 8th United States Army Air Force could muster but a dozen B-17 heavy bombers for its first strategic mission. By late in 1944 this same Air Force was to dispatch as many as two thousand heavy bombers and one thousand escort fighters in raids on any target of its choosing in enemy territory, and almost half of those were to be rail facilities. It was recognized by both sides early in the conflict that vulnerable railroad installations, particularly bridges, yards, and engine terminals, were to be primary military targets; for all of the warplanes, ships, guns, and tanks a nation could produce were useless if they could not be delivered to the troops or, once at the front, could not be operated for lack of fuel, ammunition, and spare parts.

At the risk of appearing pro-Axis (which, of course, it is not), this book has been written from a neutral point of view. Such Churchillian embellishments as "Nazi hordes," "heroic Allied defenders," and similar propagandistic terminology, quite understandable from those who were so personally involved in this greatest of conflagrations, will not be used here. Unlike the civilian and military leaders, virtually all military railway men were not career politicians or soldiers (their frequent lack of military bearing testified to that). Yet they often performed seemingly impossible tasks under appalling conditions and with inadequate supplies. In many instances, the credit for keeping a rail line operating belonged to both sides, for hundreds of thousands of prisoners of war were employed by their captors in railway construction and repair. In fact, some railway men actually cursed their own air power for its efficiency in creating monumental destruction for them to clean up—either as prisoners or as conquerors.

Unfortunately, the efficiency and practicality

of railroads, plus their almost universal presence, involved them to a considerable degree in the commission of atrocities. These events will be dealt with only as they apply directly to railroading.

In many categories, but particularly in the sense of railway logistics, World War II was actually two separate and often completely unrelated conflicts. The European theater of operations was, in every sense, a "railroad war," where track condition and locomotive availability figures were as vital in importance as ammunition and troop strength. In the Pacific, with such notable exceptions as India, Burma, China, Australia, the Japanese home islands, and Korea, the terrain, consisting of vast expanses of ocean separating island bases, did not lend itself to strategic railroading. If a local sugarcane railway was serviceable, it was of course utilized, but the "railroad armies" of Europe were not needed in the Pacific. For the foregoing reasons and because the only country to fight a two-theater railroad war with its domestic system was the United States, this volume will treat the European conflict first, then will cover the fascinating and sometimes primitive Far East, with a final capitulation of the events at the end of the war in Europe.

The title *Steel Rails to Victory* was chosen because it actually applies to both sides and because the word "victory," with its V symbol, is closely associated with World War II. Indeed, that word may have completely disappeared from at least the United States government lexicon since the war of the 1940's, while America's adversaries continue to revere it as an article of faith. Early in the war, when the Axis powers became fatally inebriated at the fountain of Nike, they supplied many pictures to neutral sources, aside from those which later fell into Allied hands. As the war progressed, there was a marked decline in the frequency of German pictures, until in late summer of 1944 they disappeared completely. After that the Germans had more vital things than photography in mind. Similarly there was an increase in Allied photo activity as the war progressed. Extensive photography is for the time of victory, and each side enjoyed its time in turn, leaving an extensive photographic record.

Military men have always possessed an acute sense of history, partly because they realize that they are participating in events of destiny and partly because history is virtually all they have to show for their efforts. The "fruit salad" of campaign ribbons on a soldier's tunic is the portfolio of his accomplishments while serving his country. The lack of material proof of military accomplishments after the fact may be one reason for the vast photographic archives maintained by military establishments around the world.

It does not absolve the American railroad industry from condemnation for the indifference with which it recalls World War II and the memories of the gallant employees who carried its standards into battle.

In recent years the incredible disdain shown by most of the major United States railways for the heritage of the dominant role they have played in the development of the nation since the 1820's has returned to haunt them. Through disregard for public relations, and with management that all too often reacted ineptly to the challenges of twentieth-century social trends, of economics, and of legalized common thievery by all levels of government, the railroads lost their grip on the imagination of the American public. One tragic result is that although the American railroads sent over a third of a million of their finest men off to a war from which over ten thousand never returned, today, with the exception of some of the lines mentioned in this volume, they have preserved virtually nothing of the great conflict for posterity. There are few records of the battalions they fielded, the glory gained, or the men lost. Even home-front publicity photos have disappeared. The World War II veterans must be wondering if the companies that they represented so well have ever realized what they accomplished. Although there is evidence that the railways of most of the other belligerents preserved much more, the railroads of America, for the most part, couldn't care less.

The presentation of the photographs in this volume is the result of an exhaustive worldwide search by the author and many helpful interested individuals, who are acknowledged elsewhere. It is unfortunate that the very nature of the war—destruction—cut so deeply into its photographic record, especially in Japan, where virtually all the wartime negatives and prints were burned during the B-29 raids. Panicky officials, fearing the wrath of the coming occupation forces, had ample time to destroy the rest. In some instances, notably the Captured Enemy Documents section of the U.S. National Archives and the various news services, copy negatives and prints were all that was available, and so quality in reproduction was compromised. Inferior wartime film, battlefield processing of film, and inexperienced photographers also detract from picture quality, but at least something of historical significance survives of the greatest railway logistics program ever attempted. It will probably never be equaled, even should mankind blunder into yet another world war.

R. Z.

Bridgehampton, New York

Prelude to Holocaust

The railway experience of the belligerent nations of World War II had its beginnings more than a century earlier. In the case of the principal European powers, in fact, it was the fresh memories of the logistics problems of the Napoleonic wars, ending in 1815, that spurred railway developments, and the military capabilities of this revolutionary form of transport were always kept in mind. A decade after Napoleon's defeat, the first British steam locomotive was in operation, but the English, relatively secure from foreign invasion, thought little of the military possibilities of railways until they themselves constructed the world's first front-line military railroad in the Crimean War in 1855. From the inception of the steam-powered flanged wheel on steel rails, however, German military strategists were impressed with the logistical possibilities of railways in wartime. As early as 1833, two years before the construction of the first German rail line, proposals were being received by the German government stressing the military necessity of railways. Meanwhile, in France General Lamarque warned the Chamber of Deputies that the military use of railways would eventually revolutionize warfare as profoundly as did the development of gunpowder. The result of the protracted debates in both of the Rhine powers was that Germany went ahead with a

strategic development of its railways while France procrastinated. This was only the first failure of the French to understand the military implication of their own and their adversaries' rail lines. The French should have learned from their experience at the hands of the railway-oriented Germans in the Franco-Prussian War of 1870–71, but even on the eve of World War II they still failed to make maximum use of the wartime capabilities of their rail system, years after Hitler had elevated his railways to a war footing.

The parallel development of railroads in the United States was put to a severe test in the Civil War of 1861–65. So involved were the American railroads in the conflict, that the War Between the States is acknowledged by military historians as having been the first "railroad war." There were over thirty thousand miles of rail lines in service in both the North and the South at the outbreak of hostilities, and few campaigns were waged without the benefit of rail transport and railway-mounted weapons. The European leaders watched the Civil War rail operations with great interest, and the lessons learned were put to good use just five years later in the Franco-Prussian conflict. Meanwhile, Austria, Russia, Italy, and other European nations were forging alliances and vast rail networks, with perhaps only a vague

premonition of the disaster that was to envelop them in 1914.

The First World War saw the first combining of the talents of European and American military railway men. It involved most of the problems of combat damage, sabotage, shipping, misuse of rolling stock, rushing supplies from port to front lines, and most of the direct combat role of the railways which were to be seen in the Second World War. Most of the World War I lessons were forgotten and had to be relearned by the Allies in 1939–42. The Germans, however, remembered—a fact which contributed greatly to their early victories.

When Commodore Perry of the United States Navy opened Japan to trade with the West in 1853, it is intriguing to consider the fact that he greatly impressed the Japanese with a working live-steam train. The Japanese soon closed their railway technological gap of thirty years and went on to build elaborate railway systems not only in their home islands, but in Formosa, Korea, and the areas of Asia that they seized in the early stages of World War II.

Steel Rails to Absolute Power

As Adolph Hitler rapidly ascended to the heights of controlling the destiny of Germany, and eventually Europe, he laid his political and military plans with the railway situation very much in mind. Immensely popular with the railway workers as well as most of the rest of the German population in the early 1930's, Hitler received valuable support wherever trains rolled. When the World War I hero Marshal Paul Von Hindenburg died while holding the office of chancellor, the cabinet appointed Hitler to fill the job until an election could confirm their decision. Prior to this crucial election, which Hitler won by a landslide on August 19, 1934, hundreds of locomotives traveled the length and breadth of Germany with Nazi slogans lettered on their tenders. Few engine men objected to such phrases as that on a 4-6-2 passenger engine (*upper left*) which was assigned to a Berlin express. *"Ein Volk, Ein Führer, Ein Ja"* reminded all Germans to vote "One people, one leader, one yes." Less than four months later, on December 14, 1934, Hitler's private train struck a bus at high speed, killing fifteen passengers on board the bus and prompting a grade-crossing safety program. On December 7, 1835, the first small segment of railway was opened in Germany. One hundred years and one day later, Hitler attended ceremonies at Nuremberg to commemorate the anniversary. It was impressive, as a lineup of brand-new passenger locomotives (*above*), coupled pilot to tender, roared by in high-speed review, and a trainload of flag-waving excursionists (*below*) saluted Hitler, who was standing in the group at right.

Three photos, Photoworld

Two photos, Photoworld

Fortifying the Rhine

Hitler's most desperate gamble during his rise to the dominant military position in Europe occurred in 1936. On March 7 he reoccupied the Rhineland with a few under-strength divisions—virtually the entire German Army at that time. Had the French and British held their occupation posts and called Hitler's bluff, the blow to his credibility would probably have been fatal. Blind to the obvious, the Allies embarked on the disastrous "peace at any price" policy and began a withdrawal. On November 30, 1936, a contingent of French troops (*upper left*) entrained for their homeland, part of a force of sixteen thousand that had been withdrawn to that date. The French then spent five billion dollars over the next three years to erect the Maginot Line, an immense complex of fortifications, connected by underground narrow-gauge electric railways (*left*) and ultimately manned by half a million troops. On the opposite bank of the Rhine, the Germans began constructing the Siegfried Line. By October, 1938, scores of little donkey engines (*above*) were engaged in constructing the necessary earthworks. German troops rode narrow-gauge internal-combustion locomotives (*right*) to and from their subterranean positions. Already the German civilian railways were being subjected to severe tests, for more than two hundred special train movements daily were required just to supply the needs of the Siegfried Line construction.

Full-Dress Rehearsals

Often overlooked in the assessments of the Second World War were the effects of several "local" conflicts during the 1930's that became the proving grounds for new tactics and weapons and devastated large areas, killing millions of civilians and soldiers. Perhaps the most important was the Spanish Civil War (1936–39), which saw the rise to power of Generalissimo Francisco Franco. Both sides made heavy use of Spain's rail system, including the Loyalist Republican irregulars (*above*), who employed a crude combination of steel plates and mattresses to fortify a train. During the Italian invasion of Ethiopia, Benito Mussolini's troops (*left*) sang and whistled their way as they rode a train from Djibouti to Addis Ababa. The most notorious of all the shabby preliminaries to the great conflict was the partition of Czechoslovakia at the Munich Conference on September 30, 1938. The following morning Hitler, buoyed by his great triumph and a good night's sleep in his armored railway car, was greeted by Reichsmarschall Hermann Göring and Konrad Henlein (*upper right*) on the station platform in Berlin. Huge swastika banners adorned the main railway depot in Brno (*right*), the second largest Czech city, on March 22, 1939. Meanwhile, all over Germany and especially in the frontier areas, well-graded sidings and yards, laid with heavy rail, were being built with great dispatch, to the bewilderment of observers who saw no need for the facilities. Once war came, the German Army put them all to their intended uses as troop embarkation points, railway artillery positions, and storage sites.

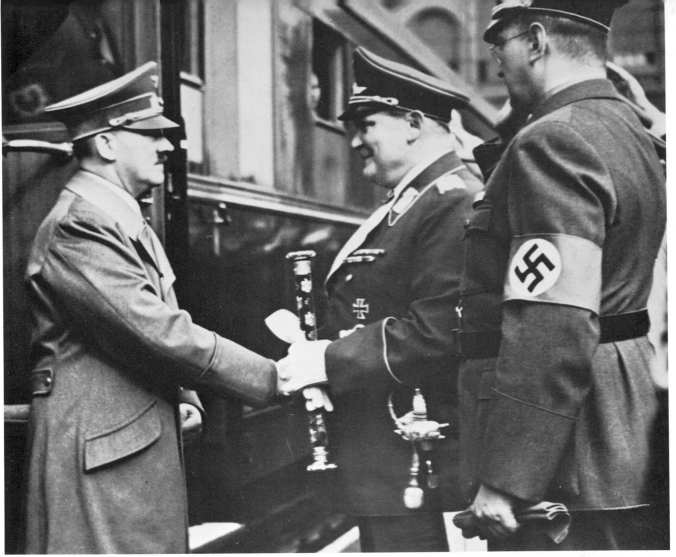

Two photos, National Archives

U.S. Army

The Irresistible Drift to Cataclysm

After signing a nonagression pact with Nazi Germany in August, 1939, Premier Josef Stalin of Soviet Russia joined in the attack on Poland, which finally made World War II official. On November 30 Stalin launched a vicious attack on hapless little Finland, but the resolute Finns, defending their homeland with a fierce determination, took a heavy toll of the invader. Thousands of fleeing Finnish civilians rode on open freight cars (*left*) for four to six days to reach the interior. In America a bitter debate raged as the nation rearmed for the coming conflict. President Franklin D. Roosevelt, defying tradition, campaigned for an unprecedented third term. It was still the era of whistle-stop politics, and on October 23, 1940, just two weeks before his election to that controversial third term, FDR (*upper left*) addressed a huge crowd in Wilmington, Delaware, from the observation platform of his campaign train. Rearmament continued at a rapidly accelerating pace as war raged across half the world. On November 3, 1941, five weeks before the Japanese attack on United States bases in the Pacific settled the issue of American participation in the conflict, the 1st Armored Division unloaded its tanks (*above*) from flatcars for maneuvers near Rock Hill, South Carolina. Southern Railway 2-8-2 locomotive No. 4612 was one of the engines assigned to hauling the M-3 medium tanks of the 69th Armored Regiment. Another series of "skirmishes" practically unobserved by the outside world occurred in Manchuria between Japanese and Russian forces. Estimates of casualties ran as high as eighty thousand annually between 1931 and 1940. Japanese troops are shown detraining (*right*) during the major clashes of mid-1939, when over twenty thousand died. In spite of the severity of the situation, Russia did not enter the Pacific war until August 8, 1945, six days before the Japanese acceptance of Allied surrender terms.

Black Star

"Blitzkrieg" Rides the Rails

After nearly a decade of preliminaries, World War II began when German armies, spearheaded by heavy armor and air attacks, swept into Poland on September 1, 1939. Within hours the Polish Air Force was destroyed on the ground and Poland's railway system was under severe attack, preventing most reserve forces from reaching the battle zones. On September 17, Russia, Hitler's recent ally, invaded Poland's almost completely unguarded east and joined forces with the Germans at Brest Litovsk the following day. Except for the resistance in Warsaw, Poland and her two-million-man army were defeated. Overall German railway strategy, which was to predominate through nearly six years of conflict, was published coincidentally at the start of the Polish invasion. Ernst Marquardt, an officer in the German Ministry of Transportation, had just completed a report entitled "Railroads in the Service of Strategy." His basic thesis was followed closely as the German Federal Railways (*Deutsche Reichsbahn*) brought all of its reserve potential into action to move the enormous daily requirement of supplies for the fifty-six divisions that were subjugating Poland. Marquardt wrote: "The railroads are best suited for mass transportation due to their large and efficient transport units. Requiring little service and providing a maximum of speed and safety, they are almost entirely independent of season and weather. They operate according to schedule and can be reached at any moment by military orders. Nothing, therefore, can replace the railroads."

It was for just those reasons that the German Air Force saw to the rapid destruction of Poland's railway network.

Although the Western Allies declared war on Germany two days after the Polish invasion, they were in no shape to battle the great German *Wehrmacht*. Through the autumn of 1939 and the following winter, Britain, France, and their allies worked desperately to prepare for a war that had already begun. Time was still on Hitler's side, however, and in the spring of 1940 it took him less than three months to seize the rest of Western Europe and pose an imminent threat to England herself. In spite of the "impregnable" Maginot Line, which was outflanked by the Germans, France fell in just a few weeks. It is interesting to note the chaotic state of the SNCF (the French National Railways) at this time. While the German Army was assigning railway battalions to work in cooperation with and under the jurisdiction of *Reichsbahn* officials, the French government was indiscriminately drafting railway men into army infantry units. This failure to grant deferments may have been more democratic than the German method of leaving the civilian railway personnel on the job, but it contributed heavily to the breakdown of the SNCF in the face of the German assault. By 1941 Hitler was well into his Balkans campaign and was making numerous inspection trips to all the conquered territories. He virtually always traveled by the safest and most secure means of transport—the railways.

Two photos, Bundesarchiv

The Defeat of Poland

Armor-plated cars and locomotives had been in use since the American Civil War, but they reached a wide-scale deployment during World War II, especially on the eastern front. A Polish armored train (*left*) was caught by *Stuka* dive-bombers and put out of action. The locomotive and tender bear a close resemblance to the streamlined passenger engines of the time. German soldiers (*above*) took inventory of goods left behind when Polish civilians allegedly robbed one of their government's side-tracked trains in September, 1939. Less than two years later, on July 3, 1941, Polish Jewish civilians (*right*) were used to unload artillery ammunition at Zamosc, southeast of Lublin, to supply the rapidly advancing *Wehrmacht* during the second week of the attack on Russia. The translation of the original German caption for this photo read: "For the first time in their lives, these Jews have to work with their hands . . . for the German Army." Once the army had moved deep into Russia and Poland had been turned over to Nazi civilian governors, the SS and other Nazi security forces rounded up hundreds of thousands of Jews and interned them in concentration camps, which few survived.

National Archives

Photoworld

Rapid Rebuilding

The Germans rehabilitated the Polish rail system so quickly that Hitler was able to make an inspection of Warsaw by train just a few days after the fall of the Polish capital. The Führer and his foreign minister, Joachim Von Ribbentrop (*left*), walk toward the shiny locomotive that was to return their train to Berlin from Warsaw. By October 19 a new railway bridge (*above*) was nearly completed over the Vistula River near Dirschau. The commander of Danzig and West Prussia, Artillery General Heitz, is shown discussing the bridge with the inspector general of railway troops. A trainload of displaced Germans from the Wolhynia area is seen crossing a bridge into the German sector of Przemysl (*below*), watched by German and Russian frontier guards, in the winter of 1939–40.

Black Star

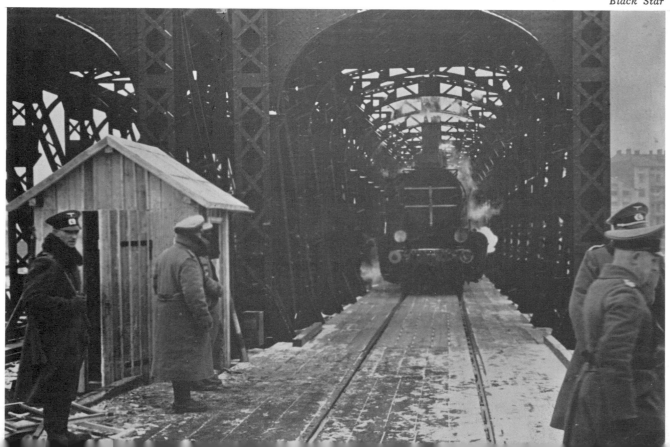

"Sitzkrieg" in the West

During the first winter of the war, action on the western front was so light that the era was referred to as the "phony war." Bored newsmen, having little more than artillery exchanges and minor small-arms fire to report, sarcastically called it a "sitzkrieg." Both sides, however, were rapidly preparing for total war. Behind the Siegfried Line many of those "useless" railroad yards that had been built in the 1930's were put to use (*left*) by units of railway artillery. The guns were spaced just far enough apart so that a direct hit by French fire could destroy only one gun. Training contin-

ued at a rapid pace. The commander of a battalion of German Army *Eisenbahnpioniere*—railway engineer troops—(*lower far left*) was showing young recruits the proper method of swinging a spike maul at Saarbrücken on March 22, 1940. Railroad activity was heavy along the upper Rhine front as light railway artillery was continually moved (*lower near left*) and dispersed for firing (*above*) along the east bank of the Rhine between Karlsruhe and Basel. The strategic railway and highway bridges at Karlsruhe (*below*) were well guarded by 3.7 centimeter antiaircraft flak guns on the banks of the Rhine.

Scandinavian Blitz

The "twilight war" ended on April 9, 1940, when German troops swept into Denmark and transport ships, loaded with soldiers and equipment, sailed into the fjords of Norway, while paratroops secured the railheads and main road junctions. So blind was the Norwegian government to the threat that when German soldiers rescued from a sunken transport announced that they were bound for Norway to protect that country from an Anglo-French attack, the Norwegians thought it was a joke! Too late Norway realized what had happened, but then the small country began to wage a spirited guerrilla campaign in the mountains. Even after the Allied force that had come to Norway's aid was withdrawn, German troops such as this squad of soldiers (*above*) had to maintain continuous patrols along the railway lines. The Germans built a new railway from Grong to Mosjoen in the summer of 1940, and on July 8 Generals Dietl, Von Rundstedt, and Von Falkenhorst, the commander of German occupation forces (*above right*), inspected the new line. At the Drontheim station (*right*) the 5th *Eisenbahnpioniere*, 2nd Regiment stood in formation to be reviewed by the generals. All of the boredom and discomfort normally associated with troop trains in any army was evident in a night move (*far right*) of a German unit between Trelleberg and Oslo on November 5, 1941.

Advance on the Low Countries

Effectively thwarted from launching a frontal attack on France across the Rhine because of the Maginot Line, Hitler swept into the Netherlands, Belgium, and Luxemburg on May 10, 1940. Within days the German Army broke through at Sedan, entering France north of the Maginot defenses. It was a time of rapid *Wehrmacht* advances, leaving the retreating Allies little time to destroy the railway lines. The *Luftwaffe*, in close coordination with the motorized thrusts of the ground forces, bombed bridges and marshaling yards and thus effectively prevented the Dutch, Belgians, and Luxemburgers from withdrawing to the Anglo-French front in northern France. German railway troops (*upper left*) are shown leaving for the front, where much repair and rehabilitation work awaited them. Soldiers en route to the western front in 1940 (*left*) sang as they rode the uncomfortable benches of a third-class coach. In the brief battle for Holland, a German machine gun crew (*above*) fired on Allied aircraft from the wreckage of railway signal towers. Ten days after the invasion of Denmark, German soldiers (*below*) stood guard with an antiaircraft gun at the approach to a Danish railroad bridge.

Two photos, National Archives

The Fall of Belgium

As German troops were occupying much of Scandinavia in April, 1940, King Leopold of Belgium ordered his railway guns (*above*) put on alert to defend the neutrality of the nation. By May 11, the day after massive *Wehrmacht* forces invaded Belgium, advancing troops were crossing a dynamited railway bridge (*lower left*) on the suspended track, while engineers had already begun to effect repairs. At Arlon on May 11 (*lower right*) and at an unidentified Belgian village on May 22 (*opposite, above*) German patrols made good use of motorized rail cars. Men of a propaganda company (*opposite, below*) secured their flower-bedecked vehicles as they prepared to leave by rail for the western front in 1940. The swastika and eagle symbol of the *Deutsche Reichsbahn* (*right*) showed clearly on the locomotive cab.

Two photos, Photoworld

Battle of the Railway Guns

During the century in which railways completely dominated the transportation planning of the industrial nations, the obvious logistics role of rails in wartime was simultaneously complemented by an evolving direct-combat mission. As the design of cannon became more sophisticated, the sheer size and weight of the guns made mobility extremely difficult. Winding dirt or mud roads traversed by horses and early motor vehicles just could not handle the rapidly accelerating artillery technology. By World War I many of the largest guns, including the famous German "Big Bertha" which shelled Paris from a range of seventy-five miles, were mounted on railway carriages. This system not only increased the mobility of the guns, but made the artillery battalion supply officer's job a relatively simple task. When the preparations for World War II began in the mid-1930's, railway guns once again figured prominently in the plans of the future belligerents, resulting in heavy use in the early stages of the conflict. By the end of the war, however, the concept of railway artillery was virtually extinct; indeed American forces, with their superior highway prime movers, had already discarded these weapons. Tactical air power and rapid armored thrusts also finished the big rail guns, for if the track was bombed behind the gun in conjunction with a tank or motorized infantry attack, it was doomed to capture or destruction. Backing up the static Maginot and Siegfried lines in 1940, however, the reliable, mobile, easily supplied heavy railway cannon were ideal weapons. On January 18, 1940, as an integral part of Maginot Line defenses, the French pressed huge four-hundred-millimeter guns into service (*above and below*) that were as big as the heaviest World War II battleship guns. Six months later the Germans captured the factory that built these monsters intact, including several brand-new units that had not even been delivered to the French Army. The loud noise and the danger of the big weapons' possibly exploding caused the crews of German 240-millimeter railway artillery (*lower right*) to stand back during firing and then to run forward to reload. These photos were made in France in 1940. When an army is relatively secure in its position and enjoys at least tactical parity in the air, as did the Germans in France prior to D-Day, railway heavy artillery, such as the 240-millimeter gun (*upper right*), can be employed even under the circumstances of modern warfare. Here the moment of firing was captured by a German Army photographer, as a railway gun shelled England from a railhead on the Channel coast of France.

"Phony War" Becomes Very Authentic

Three French soldiers (*above*) struggled to coax a squea-mish horse into a boxcar in the early days of the war. Action on the western front was so light at the time that it was not until March 5, 1940, six months after England de-clared war, that the first British prisoners were taken by the Germans (*right*) and marched into captivity along the railroad tracks in Oberesch. By May 31, however, thou-sands of their comrades had been taken and some of the survivors of the Dunkirk evacuation celebrated with fresh fruit and biscuits (*below*) at Addison Road Station upon their return to England.

France Capitulates

It took only six weeks for the armed might of the *Wehrmacht* to roll through the Low Countries and to bring the French Army to the surrender table, forcing England out of Western Europe in the process. Those incredible weeks in May and June of 1940 saw immense railroad activity and a great number of military missions directed against the railroads of France. The *Luftwaffe* struck at such lucrative targets as a French ammunition train, which was still smoking (*below*) when German ground forces reached it, and key yards and junctions, such as the depot at Aillevillers (*left*), which was hit by *Stuka* dive-bombers. Here an *Eisenbahnpioniere* officer, blueprints in hand, surveys the damage that his unit would have to clean up. French refugees, unable to escape the German advance, crowded the platforms at Orléans (*above*) while a locomotive, built in America during World War I, stood idly by in the background.

The Humiliation of France

Perhaps the most demeaning event to grate on the German national psyche was the World War I armistice agreement of 1918. Fully cognizant of this fact, the Nazi leadership staged a brilliant propaganda coup, at once avenging the earlier capitulation of Germany and exposing the pride of the vanquished French people to a terrible degra-dation. The railroad dining car in which French Marshal Ferdinand Foch had dictated the armistice terms to Germany twenty-two years earlier had been enshrined in a granite mausoleum as part of a national monument in the forest of Compiègne. Hitler ordered the car to be rolled out into the middle of the park, enabling the corps of foreign newsmen ample opportunity to cover the

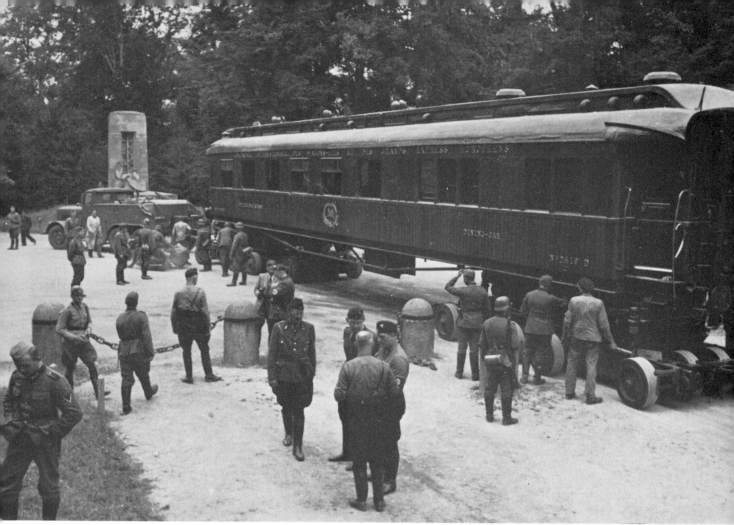

Bundesarchiv

event. Then, on June 22, 1940, while Hitler sat in Marshal Foch's chair in the famous railway car (*above left*), General Wilhelm Keitel, supreme commander of the German armed forces, read the terms of unconditional surrender to the defeated French leaders. Reichsmarschall Hermann Göring, resting his famous jeweled baton on the table, sat at Hitler's right hand. Others present included Foreign Minister Von Ribbentrop (back to camera), Admiral Raeder (far left), Von Brauchitsch, and Rudolph Hess (facing camera). The French generals, still stunned by the swiftness of their defeat, were seated at right. They included General of Aerial Warfare Bergeret and General Huntzinger (wearing dark uniform). A few minutes after the curt ceremonies, Hitler, with Göring to his left (wearing white hat), and his generals marched from the car (*lower left*) while an army band played the German national anthem, "*Deutschland über Alles.*" On Hitler's orders the entire World War I memorial park at Compiègne was destroyed and plowed under by bulldozers, except for a statue of Foch, whom Hitler grudgingly admired. The historic railway car was loaded onto highway movers (*above*) and towed away by a heavy German Army tractor. Shortly thereafter, car No. 2419D was on main line rails once more (*below*) en route to Germany, where it was viewed by the populace as a symbol of the newfound glory of the German nation. As often occurs in the course of

warfare, irony settled the score. During one of the massive Allied bombing raids, which eventually helped to bring the Third Reich down to defeat from within, the surrender railway car, by then one of the great historical treasures of Europe, was totally demolished.

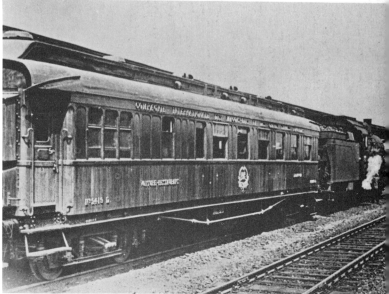

National Archives

Bundesarchiv

Four photos, National Archives

The Occupation Begins

Four long years of German occupation of France began with the surrender ceremonies at Compiègne. German troops started the take-over by putting captured French railway guns (*upper left*) to use as clothes lines. So rapidly did the German *Eisenbahnpioniere* succeed in rehabilitating the main lines of the SNCF that on July 18, 1940, Dr. Julius H. Dorpmüller, Hitler's minister of transport and former superintendent of the German Federal Railways, was able to journey to Paris to praise the *Wehrmacht* railway troops for their early successes. Addressing the assembled soldiers from the cab of an early steam locomotive preserved for historical purposes in Paris' Northern Depot (*above*), Dorpmüller exchanged Nazi salutes with the men. Work on the French railways was carried on by German engineers (*above right*); French military prisoners (*right*); and youths of the National Socialist Labor Corps (*below*), shown here using a light railway to construct a fighter base at Poix, near Amiens, for defense against Royal Air Force attacks, on September 17, 1940. Immediately after the French surrender, hundreds of thousands of French soldiers were shipped by rail to internment camps in Germany. While one German officer chased civilians away (*left*), another strutted past a group of prisoners who contemptuously stuck their tongues out at him as they prepared to entrain for years of captivity.

Bundesarchiv

37

Occupation Exercises

During the German invasion of France, Italy occupied southern portions of the country. Von Rundstedt's command train (*lower left*) was spotted at a station in the French Alps while the German general met with Italian officers to discuss occupation policies. With maps of conquered France before them (*left*) Von Rundstedt (fourth from right) and his staff discussed the situation with the Italians inside the train. Throughout the ensuing occupation, the *Wehrmacht* continually held maneuvers on French soil. On board a lightly armored train (*right*) the crew of a two-centimeter flak gun practiced firing. A machine gun squad (*below*) was entraining into an armored troop carrier in the same train.

Four photos, Bundesarchiv

A Reversal of Roles in the French Resistance

In the course of modern warfare one power continually tries to disrupt the other's railroads through the use of air power, sabotage, and ground attacks. The rail system so assaulted makes every attempt to keep operating. Once a nation is occupied by a foreign power, however, the roles are immediately reversed, as the Germans found out when they tried to keep the French railways running under the mounting French resistance, which consisted of guerrilla attacks, sabotage, and communication that kept the RAF informed of lucrative rail targets. While the Germans were using electric locomotives (*above*) to weight-test a new bridge and were decorating French locomotives (*below*) to inaugurate service across such bridges, members of the French Underground (*upper right*), armed with submachine guns stolen from the Germans or air-dropped by the Allies, planted explosives under the rails of other bridges. Just a few days after the surrender, when General Charles de Gaulle urged France to fight on, railway workers began their long battle to harass the invader. A coin dropped in the bottom of a lubricator would cause a locomotive journal to burn out. Sand in

the machinery could sideline an engine for days. Low water levels would crack boiler shells. French dispatchers would garble train orders or "accidentally" reroute trains onto the wrong lines, delaying war material for six to twenty hours at a stretch. If an especially vital shipment appeared on a division, the Resistance was informed, and as a result there might be sabotage or even armed attacks to destroy the train. As early as November, 1940, a train of cattle cars carrying French prisoners of war to German labor camps was attacked by French guerrillas who had the full cooperation of the crew, which applied the brakes at the proper moment, so that hundreds of prisoners escaped. In July, 1941, loyal French rail workers were recruited into an underground organization called "Combat," which operated under the code name "Cou-Cou." For three years "Cou-Cou" wreaked havoc with rail operations in France, seriously hampering the German war effort. Their members would send a locomotive at high speed head-on into an ammunition train, or start fires in signaling centers. The greatest effort was always made to warn the train crews in advance, so that they could jump clear. From 1941 to 1944 the combined efforts of the SNCF workers and the armed Resistance resulted in 4,208 separate acts of sabo-

tage by explosives, 1,392 derailments, and 1,817 other acts of sabotage that destroyed 2,709 locomotives, 1,721 passenger cars, and 10,591 freight cars. Among the thousands of French rail workers arrested, almost 2,000 died: 809 shot by their captors and 1,157 in concentration camps. Still, the routine of occupation continued (*below*) with the unloading of the *Wehrmacht's* daily mail from the morning train. "All the Comforts of Home" was the caption of the German cartoon showing a railway soldier arriving for a long tour of duty in Vichy-governed France.

National Archives

"Spring Voyage to the Unknown"

There were many intriguing aspects to railway operations during the era of the Third Reich that went far beyond the mysterious activities normally associated with such trains as *The Orient Express*. Trains of sealed boxcars, heavily guarded, foul-smelling, and emitting muffled sobs, rumbled through long European nights. Fast passenger locomotives, traveling at speeds over one hundred miles per hour, whisked kings, dictators, and chancellors to meetings where the destinies of entire populations were at stake. Massive one-way movements of troops and weapons foretold major battles to come. So it was that on April 30, 1941, German troops in France began a partial withdrawal, leaving a powerful, but greatly reduced, occupation force behind. Nurses from a German "soldier's home" (equivalent of the American United Service Organization) bade farewell to soldiers (*above*) as they entrained at Rouen. The original German caption for this picture referred to these troops embarking on an exciting "spring voyage to the unknown." Exciting it was to be—and disastrous, for Hitler's greatest mistake, the invasion of Soviet Russia, was just seven weeks in the future. The German forces that stayed behind in France, such as the radio operator in an armored train (*below left*) in 1942, faced the dull, although less dangerous, routine of occupation duty. Spanish volunteers of Spain's famed "Blue Division" (*below right*) were greeted by German Army nurses at a French station on their way to fight alongside German troops on the eastern front in 1942. The route card on their coach showed the train's destination: Anhalter depot, Berlin's largest railway terminal.

Two photos, Bundesarchiv

The Balkans Campaign

If most of the action of World War II in 1940 occurred on the western front, it shifted quickly toward the east by the end of the year. In September King Carol of Rumania abdicated his throne under pressure of territorial demands from Hitler's allies, Russia, Hungary, and Bulgaria. His subjects were furious that after being bled white to pay huge defense expenditures, they were now being asked to surrender to Axis and Communist demands without offering any resistance. King Carol and his entourage boarded the royal private railway car in Bucharest, and the special train careened at top speed toward the political sanctuary of Yugoslavia. All along the line Carol's former subjects fired at the train, shattering windows, pockmarking the armored royal car, and wounding the locomotive fireman. At Timisoara Carol's enemies commandeered a locomotive and pursued the royal train in a hail of gunfire. Carol beat them across the border and escaped. The spring of 1941 presented Hitler with a dilemma. Mussolini, having bungled his attack on Greece, began begging Hitler for assistance. With the assault on Russia just weeks away, thousands of German troops had to be diverted to the Balkans campaign to secure the southern flank and advance the upper pincer of the envelopment which was planned for the Suez Canal and the Middle East oil fields, in conjunction with the advance of Rommel's *Afrika Korps*. In April, 1941, a *Wehrmacht* expeditionary force was advancing along a railway line (*upper right*) toward Athens, spearheaded by the 5th *Panzer* Division. When roads were poor, clogged with refugees or rubble, and bridges blown, as frequently occurred in Greece, German motorized units found that railway rights-of-way were better suited for advancement. On April 17, during the heavy fighting, German railway and labor troops (*lower right*) were well on the way to returning a blasted Greek tunnel to service. The way to Greece had been cleared for Germany a few weeks earlier when Hitler's demands on the Yugoslav government that the German Army be granted the right to operate "supply trains" across Yugoslavian rail lines were met by a pro-Axis regime, which appropriately traveled by steam train to Vienna to sign the necessary documents. Yugoslavia rode the rails to Nazi domination, but as in France a strong resistance movement soon became active. In what has been referred to as "virtually a race between the Germans, the Allied air forces, the National Army of Liberation and the Partisan units" World War II took a heavy toll of Yugoslavia's railways: 56 per cent of the tracks, 80 per cent of the locomotives, 90 per cent of all rolling stock, 61 per cent of large bridges and viaducts, and 55 per cent of smaller bridge structures.* In Greece the damage was more severe, including the blasting of huge viaducts by British paratroopers working with Greek guerrillas. One of these, the Asopos Viaduct, took the Germans two months to repair, working continuously with thousands of Greek and Polish laborers. The first train to cross the repaired span fell through, taking much of the bridge with it. The laborers had sabotaged the repair work! Adolph Hitler's fifty-second birthday, in April, 1941, was celebrated by the Führer in his private command car with his generals and top Nazi leaders while he was directing the Balkan campaign, at the height of his power.

* *Railways in Wartime*, E. F. Carter, Fred. Muller, Ltd., p. 194.

National Archives

Fascist Leaders Meet at the Station

With air transport still somewhat unreliable and with the distinct dangers of aircraft's being downed by enemy craft or even by friendly antiaircraft which had been misinformed, Europe's leaders usually chose the eminently safer and more comfortable first-class passenger trains when traveling on their various missions of world importance. When Francisco Franco, victor of the Spanish Civil War, finally paid a state visit to meet his benefactor, Hitler, in Germany, it was by rail. The German Führer greeted Franco in the vestibule of the latter's private car (*left*) and the Spanish officers (*right*) on the red-carpeted station platform. Although there was much collaboration between the ideological comrades, including the sending of the "Blue Division" to the eastern front, Franco wisely stayed out of the war and withdrew his volunteers from the east in 1943. He was the only fascist leader to survive the war. In February, 1941, when Mussolini—shown at left (*above*) marching down a station platform in Munich with Hitler—met with Franco on the Italian Riviera, he tried to draw Spain into the war against the Allies, who were dealing him heavy blows in Greece and North Africa. Under the guns of an Italian armored train whose turrets were continually traversing the Mediterranean as it chugged along the coast, Franco politely expressed his gratitude for past favors and remained neutral in the war. The train may have been the heavily armored antiaircraft train that Hitler had given to *Il Duce* on the Italian dictator's fifty-fifth birthday in 1938.

Hitler Rides the Rails

A special detachment of SS troops (*left*) always guarded Hitler's train. When Finland's Marshal Baron Mannerheim and President Risto Ryti were visited by Hitler (*above*) on Mannerheim's seventy-fifth birthday, June 6, 1942, they toured Finnish defenses by rail. Hitler's early popularity among Germans was evident whenever he appeared at the windows (*below*) of the trains he rode, such as these scenes at Wilhelmshaven on June 17, 1936. Hitler's wartime armored command car was bullet- and bombproof, watertight, and heavily padded inside. The bullet-resistant windows could be automatically covered with heavy steel shutters in seconds. Recent medical studies of the adverse effects of air travel on the human physical processes lend credence to the theory that British Prime Minister Neville Chamberlain, who always met with Hitler after exhausting flights from England, was never in any condition to bargain with the Führer, who had arrived in Munich relaxed and refreshed in his comfortable railway car.

National Archives

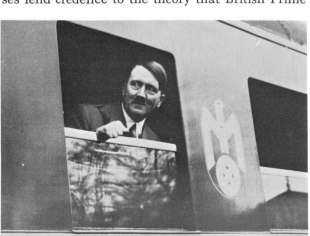

Cataclysm in the East

At two o'clock in the early morning of June 22, 1941, a Russian locomotive with a red star emblazoned on its smokebox front chugged through the forests and along the banks of the Bug River in Poland. It slowed, then halted at a small guardhouse. German soldiers, unusually alert on such a sultry June night, exchanged greetings with the Russian crew and Red Army troops guarding the train, which contained Ukrainian grain bound for Germany. After a quick look at the conductor's bill of lading, the train was waved through. A few yards away, on both sides of the tracks, ranks of German soldiers crouched breathlessly in trenches. Behind them tanks, artillery, and all the support units for the largest invasion in history were poised. Less than an hour after the Russian train passed through the border post, a force of three million Germans and Axis allies, including two hundred combat divisions, attacked the Soviet Union on a thousand-mile front which extended from the Baltic to the Black Sea.

Stalin had been so preoccupied with building up his armed forces, economy, and transportation networks for a strike at Germany, that he ignored the warnings from British Prime Minister Winston Churchill and his own intelligence that he was about to be "outscoundreled" by Hitler. Scores of trainloads of oil, minerals, grain, cotton, and other strategic goods rolled daily from Russia to Germany. Stalin's total disregard for the plight of England in supplying this vast material to Germany vanished overnight, literally, when he immediately demanded that Britain invade *Festung Europa*—Hitler's Fortress Europe—to divert the *Wehrmacht* from its latest, boldest, and costliest venture. Stalin conveniently forgot, or didn't care, that it was Russian oil that had played a major role in running England off the Continent in the first place.

The first few weeks of the mammoth invasion in the East, code-named Operation Barbarossa by the Germans, went smoothly enough. Virtually the entire world believed that the Germans would claim total victory by autumn. The attack fanned out into three main thrusts along a front which had lengthened to nearly two thousand miles as the *Panzer* spearheads neared their prime objectives. Army Group North reached the outskirts of Leningrad on schedule. Army Group Center rolled relentlessly toward Moscow, capturing Smolensk during the

first month. Army Group South, which Hitler considered the most important, drove into the Ukraine and toward the Caucasus oil fields for the eventual closing of the pincers on the Middle East. Hitler came within just a few miles, and in the case of Leningrad, within a few thousand yards, of all three objectives. This failure to win the war in the East before the entry of the United States into the conflict and the onset of the worst winter in a century in December, 1941, resulted in almost four years of a war of attrition unsurpassed in history, which proved to be the decisive factor in the defeat of Germany.

With victory within his grasp, Hitler vacillated, ignoring the advice of his generals on what was largely a railroad issue. The experience of the *Wehrmacht* during the early weeks of the campaign showed that the primitive roads of Russia could not support modern armies, especially with the coming of the rains in autumn, which turned the roads into quagmires. Therefore *the most vital military objective on both sides on the eastern front was the highly developed rail network.* Because of this, the German high command urged that Army Group Center be given priority for its drive on Moscow, which was literally the hub of the railways of the USSR. The capture of the capital would mean the interdiction of virtually every railway line west of the Ural Mountains, where most of Russia's population and industry were situated. By the time Hitler realized this, the Soviet forces had gained the necessary time to organize a successful defense of Moscow.

Millions of people who had been under Soviet domination had hailed the Germans as liberators. Here Hitler made another grave error. Since the Russians were considered racial inferiors, they were brutally suppressed by the SS and the Nazi civil administrators. Most Russians finally decided that a home-grown regime that thrived on the misery of its subjects was preferable to a foreign one and rose up to fight the invader. If the Germans had problems with the French Resistance destroying railway facilities, the activity of Russian guerrillas was a constant nightmare by comparison. More than in any other area of combat operations, the fortunes of World War II rode the rails on the eastern front.

Direct Combat Support by Rail

A ten-drivered Russian road engine is shown pushing a trainload of camouflaged tanks right up to the front in September, 1941, when Hitler's indecision had slowed the German assault even more than had the stiffening Red Army resistance. So close did this locomotive operate to German positions that a heavier flatcar, carrying a T-34 tank—one of the best of the war—was semipermanently coupled to the engine to protect the rail link in the event of a German attack.

Two photos, National Archives

Stalin's Message and Other Problems

In calling the Russian people to rise up as one to battle the Germans, Stalin issued the famous scorched-earth policy of denying the invaders anything that might be of any use to them. It is significant that Stalin stressed the importance of trying to save all railway rolling stock in his most famous speech. What railway equipment they could not keep behind their lines the Russians destroyed. More often than not, German assault troops found trains on fire (*right*) or wrecked. A direct hit from a *Luftwaffe* light bomb halted a Russian armored train (*above right*), resulting in its capture. So rapid at times was the German advance that much railway equipment was captured, such as a red-starred locomotive (*left*) with steam up, which was decorated with a swastika flag by its captors. A German infantryman found Red Army General Rothberg (*above*) wounded and hiding behind a locomotive during the battle for Rezekne, Latvia, on July 13, 1941. One of the Germans' biggest railway problems lay in the fact that the Russian railways are of a broader (five-foot) gauge than those of Western Europe. This meant switching loads, changing track gauge, and other engineering problems. The Baltic States, for example, were divided as follows: Lithuania, standard gauge; Latvia, standard and Russian; Estonia, Russian gauge.

Difficult Advance on Moscow

To circumvent the difficulties presented by the dirt roads of Russia, German mechanized columns frequently turned to railroad rights of way, as they had in Greece several months earlier. After laying timbers on the tracks of a railway trestle (*left*), German troops nearly got a self-propelled cannon across before one of its caterpillar tracks slipped off. Other guns in the unit were waiting on the opposite bank to cross. On the alert against strafing Russian attack planes, an antiaircraft crew (*above*) guarded a supply train. The effectiveness of *Blitzkrieg* tactics was again proved in Russia as swarms of *Stukas* cleared heavy resistance pockets before the advancing armor and infantry thrusts. The dive-bombers also found lucrative rail targets; they scored a direct hit on a tank riding a flatcar (*below*) near Smolensk on July 24, 1941.

National Archives

Three photos, Bundesarchiv

General Mud and General Winter

Dating back to Napoleon's invasion of Russia in 1812 (a discomfiting historical parallel which rightfully haunted the *Wehrmacht* high command), the Russians have always felt that they have two great allies in the very nature of their homeland: General Mud and General Winter. In view of their service in World War II, both "generals" deserve to be promoted to field marshals. The Germans who unloaded gasoline at a forward depot (*above*) and who had to free trains frozen to the rails in deep snow, like the one at Sanosnaja (*below*) on March 7, 1942, knew the wrath of nature's generals. The Germans made good use of both broad-gauge railway lines (*upper left*) and narrow-gauge tracks (*lower left*) to move their artillery to the front. During the Russian campaign the Germans requisitioned equipment from all over occupied Europe to operate on the Soviet railways. French, Italian, Greek, Polish, Hungarian, Dutch, and German cars wound up in Russia, as did the rolling stock of a half-dozen other nations.

National Archives

Off-Beat Motive Power

Because of the thoroughness with which the Russians removed or destroyed railway motive power in the path of the German advance, and the shortage of operating railway personnel and the poor condition of much of the Russian railroad track, the *Wehrmacht* often had to turn to ingenuity to put railway lines to use. Small units of motive power served other useful functions, doing duty as reconnaissance and patrol cars. It would be difficult for a steam locomotive to "sneak up" undetected on anything, but a little motor car, such as the one transporting an armed engineer reconaissance patrol in Lepel (*left*) was more flexible. It could even be removed from the track by the crew in the event of enemy activity or an oncoming train. This patrol was searching for breaks in the line on July 18, 1941, and was to report its findings to the *Eisenbahnpioniere* commander for action. These little cars required only small amounts of fuel and virtually no maintenance. By the spring of 1943 the Germans were in a general retreat, their resources getting critically low. The motorcycle patrol car at Gorki (*upper left*) and the twin bicycle affair (*above*) at Pustinka are indicative of the austerity that began determining German policy in the fourth year of World War II. Back in August, 1941, the Germans had few locomotives to operate on Russian broad-gauge tracks at Schepetowka, so they put Russian Army prisoners (*above right*) to work as switch engines. As the Germans advanced through the Pripet Marshes, using the solid embankments of railway lines, the Russians met them with armored automobiles converted to railroad use, such as this one (*right*) which was captured by the Germans.

56

Two photos, Bundesarchiv

German Army Railway Engineers Up Front

Still covered with withered camouflage branches and pockmarked by heavy-caliber bullets and shrapnel, a Russian locomotive was being inspected by two German railway engineers (*left*) preparatory to repairing it for *Wehrmacht* service. Russian prisoners (*above*) unloaded new rails. On the day of the capture of Lepel, an *Eisenbahnpioniere* officer (*right*) was checking a switch while an infantryman kept a sharp vigil for snipers. Painted white for winter camouflage, a German *Panzer* V tank (*below*) was unloaded from a flatcar.

Guarding the long, lonely lines of communication in Russia during the first winter of the war, a German soldier looked warily down the snow-covered tracks that stretched endlessly through forests and over barren steppes to his homeland, 1,300 miles over the horizon. At any moment, the intense boredom could be broken by the shattering roar of a strafing Stormovik or the crash of a sniper's bullet, making him just another one of the three million who would never return. What was he thinking now, of the war, the cold, his family, his Führer. . . ?

The Bleak, Deadly Russian Front

The enormity of the titanic struggle between the two most powerful armies in the world up to that time may never be known, even to those who fought it. The major strength of Germany's nine million military personnel had been hurled upon a waiting but ill-prepared armed force of ten million Soviet troops. Because of the very nature of the war—total, brutal, distant from communications, a war waged by two totalitarian powers whose every news release was suspect—many statistics and recollections were lost almost as soon as they occurred. The figures that did reach the outside world were so staggering as to be meaningless: in the first three months, Stalin had lost over 2½ million men, almost 20,000 tanks, 22,000 guns, and 15,000 aircraft! Later, as the tide of battle swept the Germans back, their losses mounted, but they continued to exact a much greater toll from the Russians. The frightful tales of brutality on both sides, of entire nonbelligerent populations being decimated, of fronts so fluid that attacking divisions found themselves enveloped and annihilated by a retreating enemy, slowly trickled out to an anxious world. By the time it was all over in 1945, almost three million German soldiers—5 per cent of the total population of Germany—had perished on the Eastern Front alone in combat, from exposure to the elements, or in Soviet prison camps. Through it all, the Russian railways were battered but held up quite well. In fact, while Germany occupied only one tenth of Russia, she held over one third of the railways, which accounted for 40 per cent of all train movements in prewar days. The Russians had lost only 15 per cent of their locomotives to the invaders and were able to save so many cars as to have a surplus even during some of the most critical times. The Russian railways survived every test, including the movement of entire industrial complexes from the west to the Urals, which enabled Russia to carry on the war. All Soviet railway workers were drafted and put under martial law; the result was precise military control of the vital transport network, including an automatic capital charge of treason for the many railway workers who collaborated with the Germans in the forlorn hope that they were being liberated.

Stalin Strikes Back

Although weakened by Stalin's insane purge of the late 1930's, low in morale from the debacle in Finland, and unprepared for the magnitude of the German invasion, the Red Army managed to regain much of its effectiveness by the end of 1941. Forced to apply the old Russian tactic of retreating hundreds of miles to lure a confident enemy deep into the country, then using the very basic elements of distance, weather, and terrain to their advantage, Soviet generals began to exploit weaknesses of the *Wehrmacht*. Early in 1942, a trainload of armor (*above*) was en route to the front and a winter-camouflaged Red trooper (*below*) stood guard over the bodies of German soldiers killed during the attack that had captured their train. Armed with submachine guns, Soviets flattened themselves on a partially destroyed railroad track (*upper right*) as a German shell exploded a few yards in front of them.

Four photos, Sovfoto

Nine Hundred Days of Disaster for Leningrad

When the German Army Group North smashed through to the suburbs of Leningrad in August, 1941, the first determined resistance of the Russian people finally threw the Nazi timetable of conquest off schedule. For almost two and a half years, the Germans laid siege to "the cradle of Bolshevism," which Hitler intended to destroy completely. Over half a million Leningraders assisted in the construction of defenses that held. Cut off from all sources of supply until Lake Ladoga froze solid enough to support sleighs and later trucks, approximately one million of the city's inhabitants starved to death. Had it not been for the rail lines, however, the entire city would have perished and the defense would have collapsed. The main railway line from the southeast brought supplies to the lake. During the second winter of siege, tracks were actually laid over the ice, but hardly used, because a Red Army counterattack, which captured the shoreline only five hundred yards from German guns, enabled a permanent railway to be built to the city. Trains crept in only at night and the line was cut over 1200 times by artillery in 1943, when 4.5 million tons of freight was delivered. Earlier in the war all of the museum treasures had been removed by armored train, and before the electric power was lost, thousands of soldiers and civilian volunteers rode directly into battle in the city's trolley cars, whose farthest terminals were actually in disputed territory. By the spring of 1942 little switching locomotives (*below*) hauled carloads of life-giving bread flour along the streetcar tracks of the city that almost died.

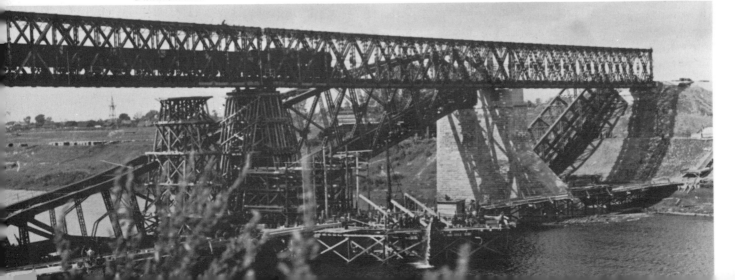

Bundesarchiv

German Ingenuity Bridges the Gaps

In Russia the German engineer *Eisenbahnpioniere* units found that although a considerable number of bridge structures had been wiped out by both the *Luftwaffe* and the fleeing Communists, their own ability to repair the damage almost always kept railway lines open to the front. Two impressive accomplishments were the methods used to span blown masonry arches through the expedient of extending I beams from one side, sliding the bridge girders across, and withdrawing the beams (*upper left*), and a daring 320-foot free span (*left*) used to bridge a tributary of the Bug River at Nikolaev, on the Black Sea, in 1943. During the initial assault, standard Roth Wagner bridging (*lower left*) was used, as were all-timber bridges (*above*) and timber and steel combinations (*below*). Note the use of converted army trucks as construction locomotives.

Pionier-Schule

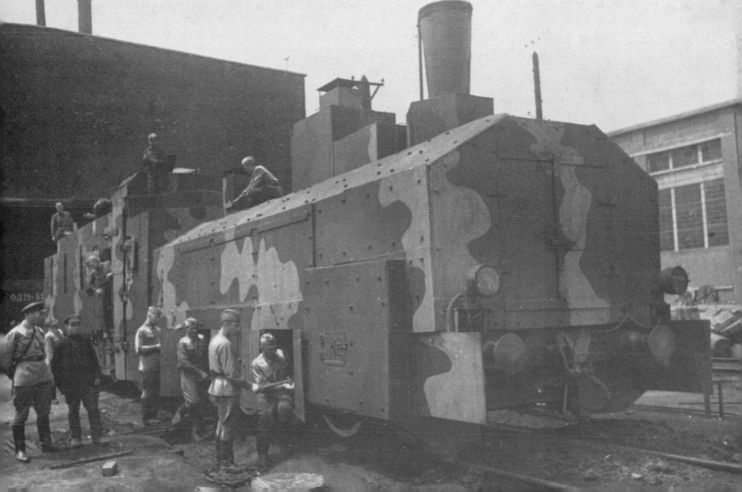

Weird Monsters of the Rails

Of all the strange equipment seen on the railways of the world during almost a century and a half of railroading, perhaps none has surpassed the phenomenon of the armored train. Dating back to the American Civil War, when cannon were mounted on heavy flatcars and protected by thick iron plates, the doctrine of the armored train was refined under fire in several wars during the next eighty years. The status of transportation and weaponry technology by the beginning of World War II together created a "golden age" of the armored train during that time, particularly on the eastern front. Unlike the huge railway guns, whose usefulness was on the wane, the speedy armored trains were, in effect, tanks of the rails. One prime mover could bring the fire power of an entire platoon of tanks, as well as a machine gun platoon, into a combat situation where railroad tracks were serviceable. With the bad road conditions of Russia, these trains assumed great strategic importance. The varied construction and degrees of impregnability of the armored trains greatly enhanced their interest. Although there were a few standard designs, especially on the German side, many armored trains were one-of-a-kind, on-the-spot creations, built in local factories or railway shops, almost as spare-time projects. Bristling with antiaircraft cannon, machine guns, and light artillery pieces, armored trains were suited for a variety of missions, including fire support, escort of important train moves, guarding and patrolling, and when carrying infantry, limited attack roles. Some armored trains, especially those erected in tank foundries, had mechanized revolving gun turrets. At Odessa in October, 1941, a Stalin-musta-

Imperial War Museum

chioed old foreman (*upper left*) was checking his work sheets as a crew armor-plated an old locomotive. Soviet troops (*lower left*) are seen familiarizing themselves with a newly armored engine while their commander discussed the project with a foreman. Many Russian workers labored after hours to build these trains, including the railway men of the capital, who donated the armored cars of the train *Moscow* (*above*) to the Red Army. When the railway shop workers of Moscow presented an armored train to army officers (*below*) in March, 1942, they lettered the slogan "Death to German Occupiers" on the flanks of one car.

Three photos, Sovfoto

Railway Firepower

En route to the front, spotters in an armored train antiaircraft turret (*left*) searched for German planes. In case of a heavy attack on the train, the guncrew could retract the quadruple machine gun mount and slide shrapnel-proof covers over their turret. In August, 1941, antiaircraft guns on a well-camouflaged armored car (*above*) prepared to open fire on German bombers, while the commander of an armored train (*right*) used the locomotive cab as a command post as he peered through binoculars for signs of enemy activity. Although much heavier than most equipment, the armored trains were well supported by the track and structures of the Russian railways. The thick armor plating, which protected locomotives, equipment, weapons, and men from shrapnel and small-arms fire, could be pierced only by direct hits from aircraft or artillery. Even if the tracks were cut in front of and behind a train, it usually had at least a few hundred yards left in which to maneuver.

Imperial War Museum

The Organization behind the Front

The German officers who planned Operation Barbarossa relied heavily on the assumption that the Russian railways would collapse under the strains of combat and of supplying the Soviet Union with all the means of waging total war. The rapid advance of the *Wehrmacht* actually served to assist the railway network, since its area of operations was greatly reduced and it did not have to serve the industries, farms, or the vast populations that came under German control. Militarizing railway workers—which included increasing their rations, fuller utilization of cars, deferred maintenance, and strict observance of preestablished priorities —contributed to disproving the German theory. The inherent economies and great flexibilities of railway transport, plus its uncanny ability to absorb the most brutal punishment, saved the situation for the Soviet government, which used its railway network with brutal efficiency in most in-

stances. The closest thing the Russians had to a standard armored railway car design was the big revolving turret car shown in action, supporting an attack (*above*) and guarding a rail yard near the front (*right*) as a trainload of artillery passed. These cars were usually coupled in pairs on either side of the locomotive. Sometimes battle wagons bristling with machine guns and antiaircraft (*right*) were at the end of the train, providing local security. Note also the battery of four machine guns on the locomotive tender. Since the engine was in the middle of the train, it was relatively secure in the event of a hit on the train. Even if the train were derailed by a mine or bridge collapse, the chances were good that the locomotive and half of the train could be saved and backed up, to return to battle later. The guns of an armored train illuminated the night (*upper right*) as they fired in support of a Russian offensive on the Leningrad front in March, 1943.

Two photos, Sovfoto

The Biggest Gun and "Slave Labor"

As in World War I, the biggest gun to see service in the second global conflict of necessity rode the

rails. A huge siege gun with extreme range and great accuracy, *Schwere Gustav* ("Heavy Gustav") or *Dora*, as it was named by its crews, played an important role in the capture of Sevastopol. It eventually wound up in the decisive battle of the European war—Stalingrad—where it poured its one-ton shells into the beleaguered Soviet fortress. As with so many aspects of the eastern front, little is known of the ultimate fate of *Gustav*. Presumably it was destroyed or captured, along with the entire German Sixth Army, on the banks of the Volga. The gun is shown here during its employment at Sevastopol. So huge that it had to be carried by a double-track railroad, *Dora* may well have been the largest cannon ever built. Much has been written of the Nazi deportation of millions of citizens from occupied countries back to the Reich to work in the factories, on transportation facilities, and in erecting defense works, such as the West Wall. That hundreds of thousands of these people suffered great privation, many perishing, is well documented, but the blanket term of "slave labor" applied by Allied propagandists was an exaggeration. As workers in the war effort, these people often received better rations than other civilians. Many of the large Soviet populations considered deportation to Germany a blessing, for they would be free of the hated Stalin regime at last. The stupidity of the Nazi authorities, who mistreated these willing potential allies, must take much of the credit for the defeat of Germany. The Nazi theories of racial inferiority did not allow for putting thousands of Russian volunteers in responsible civil and military positions. Consequently, a great reserve of talent and manpower was abused and finally alienated from the cause of German anti-Communism. Still, the German railways transported millions of laborers to all sections of occupied territory, including Russian women (*opposite*), who appeared quite content as they filled water cans and received their bread ration from German troops in a railroad yard in Russia, prior to their deportation to Germany early in the war.

Two photos, Bundesarchiv

Northern Operations

Since Germany occupied Norway and was an ally of Finland after the opening of the eastern front, Lapland, the barren northern outpost of Europe, assumed a strategic importance. It was from here that Germany received many of her natural resources and that the *Luftwaffe* operated to interdict the Allied sea lanes to Murmansk and Archangel. German and Finnish troops manned the line to thwart any Soviet invasion of the area. During the winter of 1942–43, many Russian prisoners (*above*) were brought to rear areas via the light railway that was kept open by the use of a wedge plow (*left*). The following summer the Germans used mules and horses (*opposite*) to haul supplies along a broad-gauge line in Lapland.

Four photos, Bundesarchiv

Railroading on the American

The fall of Northern Europe, the Low Countries, and France and the expected collapse of England before the seemingly invincible German forces—all within a span of just two months in the spring of 1940—resulted in a rapidly accelerated defense policy in the United States. It was immediately realized that virtually the entire logistics burden in the zone of the interior would have to be carried by the railroads. The response of America's railways can only be described as superb in terms of foresight, operations, and equipment and personnel utilization.

Despite the staggering blow of the Depression, American railways began a program of ordering thousands of new locomotives, both steam and diesel, and much rolling stock, while the manufacturers prepared to fulfill not only these unusually large requests, but orders for literally thousands of locomotives and tens of thousands of cars that would ultimately serve to tide over the recaptured railways in a score of countries, improve the capabilities of Allied railways in the combat theaters, and keep the United States lines moving until such time as the destroyed and/or captured industries in the devastated areas could begin producing again. During the war over 351,000 American railway men—about 20 per cent of the 1941 force—were called into military service; yet the American rail network moved over 90 per cent of all freight and 97 per cent of the military personnel involved in the war effort. Although the railroads lost 20 per cent of their personnel, and had to train replacements—often women—they managed to move twice the tonnage in 1943 that they had handled just six years earlier. Since railroads are the most efficient means of transport and the only form that maintains its own rights-of-way, communications, construction, and complete repair facilities, it is difficult to even begin

U.S. Army

Homefront

to understand how the monumental mission of the railways during World War II could have been conceived. The vast flexibility, inherent economy, and ability to absorb incredible abuse, coupled with a readiness to greatly expand operations, further illustrate how the rails may have succeeded. Nothing, it seems, can ever explain how they were actually able to pull it off without a single major crisis.

All during this time, it must be remembered, the railroads were called to carry a much greater load of civilian traffic resulting from the severe restrictions on all other forms of transport (including walking, for those who recall the leather shortage). By 1942 the German submarine menace had become so great that virtually all oil and most coal movements that had formerly gone by coastal shipping had to move by rail. Even the disintegration of rival forms of transport and the resultant shift of burdens to the rails had little effect on their efficiency!

Military Utility Railways—Large and Small

Because of their vast size, many installations of both the Army and the Navy had their own railroad facilities. The operation of these base lines was either performed by military rail servicemen or contracted to the civilian lines, which interchanged with the bases. Some of the light railways—narrow-gauge lines—of the First World War were still in use, such as the one at Fort Dix, New Jersey (*left*) shown here loaded with troops armed with Browning Automatic Rifles on their way to the firing range. The largest of the utility lines connected the two big Louisiana Army posts, Camp Claiborne and Camp Polk. Constructed during the winter of America's formal entry into the war, the C & P became a training facility for many units. As P-39 pursuit aircraft screamed in for a mock strafing run (*below*), infantrymen dashed for cover while an antiaircraft gun behind the locomotive swung into action. The Long Island Rail Road coaches in the train were indicative of the Army's reliance on civilian lines for equipment early in the war.

Defending the Home Front

Even before the Japanese attack on Pearl Harbor brought the United States into the conflict, internal-combustion power began to appear on the domestic military railway scene, as it already had on the civilian network. In April, 1941, the World War I light railway motive power was replaced at Fort Dix (*left*) with a Plymouth "dinkie." The charming little puffers still turned out in force on the narrow-gauge rails of Fort Benning, Georgia (*lower left*), as late as July 28 of that hectic year of rapid national mobilization. Although railway artillery played a vital role in the initial phases of the European war, the rapid advances in motorized gun mounts and airborne coastal defenses relegated this equipment to a minor role before Pearl Harbor and completely obliterated it from United States Army planning by the time of the land assaults on Axis territory. An order of railway guns was procured from the Watertown, Massachusetts, arsenal by the Coast Artillery in 1938, in one of the first acts of preparation for World War II, illustrating the importance of these guns in operational planning only three years prior to their virtual discard. These sleek, light (by European standards) eight-inch naval-type guns were mounted on carriages supported by six-wheel trucks. One of these gun cars weighed 113 tons (comparable to an average Consolidation freight engine), could fire a 200-pound shell 20 miles, and penetrate almost a foot of armor plate. A crew (*right*) is seen loading one of these guns, while two others are shown in dispersed position (*below*) along a coastal beach. The gun in the foreground was in traveling position, the one in back, its outriggers extended, was ready to

*Railroad
Magazine*

fire. For several years these guns were kept ready to repel an invasion on either coast, but as the Allies took the offensive on all fronts, they were phased out of service.

Photoworld

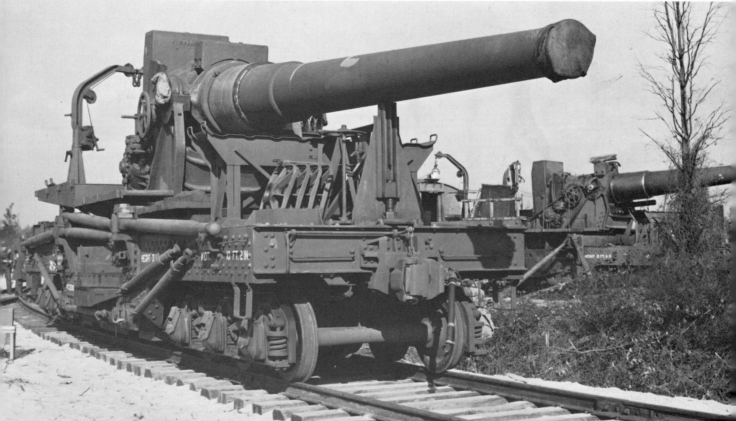

Two photos, Railroad Magazine

From Quartermaster Corps to Transportation Corps

From the experiences of World War I in France, doctrine concerning the organization and operation of the U.S. Army Military Railway Service (MRS) during World War II was formulated by military planners during the 1939–1942 period. It was found that the regimental organization was not suited for the MRS and rather than being soldiers operating trains (instead of artillery, machine guns, or trucks), the MRS was actually an American railroad (or several of them) in uniform. The distinction was more than mere semantics, for it meant that the Army realized that the skills and experience required for railway operations could not be acquired in six weeks of basic training. Certainly the Germans and Russians, among other combatants, had learned this lesson. Railways in the combat zone would be operated in the manner of the systems at home—by divisions.* To develop a military force comparable to a civilian railroad division, the concept of the Railway Operating Battalion (ROB) evolved. An ROB was divided into

* Not to be confused with military divisions.

four companies, to make a completely self-sustaining railway "division." The construction and right-of-way repairs were handled by "A" Company, consisting of two track platoons and one bridge platoon. "B" Company, responsible for keeping the equipment in running shape, had two platoons, each of which was a complete roundhouse and engine terminal force, plus a platoon for shopping the rolling stock. The largest unit in the ROB was Company "C," the operating outfit that supplied the train crews. The Headquarters and Service Company was the support unit, providing, in addition to dispatchers, telegraphers, and linemen, such essential services as supply, food, and housing for the railway troops. For additional maintenance there were shop battalions, which were comparable to the main shops of a major railroad; and the Army Corps of Engineers could be called upon to build everything from new bridges and buildings to an entire railroad, if necessary. In the Navy it was the famed Seabees who handled major railway work, which was relatively rare in the scope of Naval combat operations.

A Railway Operating Battalion consisted of as

many as 24 officers and 847 enlisted men. By the end of the war there were 38 active ROB's, plus 12 Shop Battalions † and other attached units, not to mention Engineer Construction Battalions, Signal Corps, and other support units. In addition to Headquarters, Military Railway Service, there were 10 Railway Grand Divisions (comparable to the General Offices of a civilian railroad) to supervise the aggregations of battalions. They had approximately 100 men and, in the manner of railroad General Offices, were the headquarters of the "top brass"; field grade officers were the "superintendents" and "vice-presidents," and the colonel in command could be likened to the president of a civilian line.

Because of the great reliance on railroads and the realization that World War II would indeed be a "big one," the Transportation Corps was formed in 1942, combining the former railway functions of the Corps of Engineers and the Quartermaster Corps, plus highway and some water transport. In 1942, however, the railway operations assumed paramount importance in the new corps. The photographs on these pages show motive power around the time of the founding of the Transportation Corps. What was probably the Army's first diesel locomotive (built by Alco-General Electric in January, 1941) is shown (below) in its quartermaster livery at the Holabird QM Depot in Baltimore, Maryland. Before the introduction of thousands of "standard" GI 2-8-0's, built from 1942 to 1945, the Army ordered some interesting engines, such as 2-8-0 No. 6998 (a sister of the engine that appears on page 77), of which at least six were built by Lima in 1942 (left) and 0-6-0's such as 4078 (lower left), several of which still survive on steam excursion railways in the United States. A standard Pershing engine of World War I, the 8341 (right), was named for the great commander. She was completely rebuilt at Holabird and is shown on a multigauge shop track on March 17, 1942.

† See Index for list of Railway Battalions, dates of activation, and sponsoring railroads.

Two photos, U.S. Army

GI's Workin' on the Railroad

Exactly three weeks after Pearl Harbor, paratroopers of the 502nd Parachute Battalion (*above*) were taught the rudiments of locomotive operation at Fort Benning, in case they should find an opportunity to seize enemy locomotives. Although the Southern Pacific would probably rather forget it, they did sponsor the 716th Railway Operating Battalion, which earned notoriety as the "Million Dollar Battalion" in France, a scant six months after this photo (*below*) was taken at Fort Sam Houston, Texas, on May 11, 1944. Although the shop men in this photo probably were not guilty of wrongdoing, many members of "C" Company of the 716th were court-martialed for selling supplies to French black marketeers. At first, items disappeared from cars bound for the front, then whole cars were cut out of trains and such commodities as gasoline and clothing vanished. Legend has it that before they were caught, men of the 716th diverted entire trains. Several officers received prison terms, and General Dwight D.

Two photos, U.S. Army

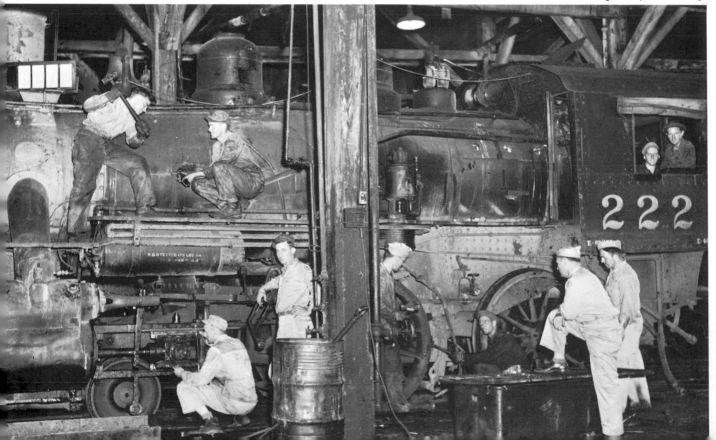

Eisenhower is said to have personally issued the order giving the guilty enlisted men the choice of prison or transfer to line units. They chose the latter, just in time for the Battle of the Bulge! It was the only serious misconduct on the otherwise magnificent record of the MRS. Although much material never reached its intended destination, this was the only instance of a mass conspiracy to sell it on the black market. Had the 716th used it themselves or given or traded it to other units, nothing would have been said. Selling the misappropriated freight to civilians, however, was considered a most serious crime.

The Crime & Punishment

When the Army activated the first of its Railway Operating Battalions for World War II on May 1, 1941, at Fort Belvoir, Virginia, it was decided that this unit—the 711th—would become the training, or cadre, battalion, from which future units would emerge. Being the first, the 711th was also one of only four ROB's without sponsorship by the United States rail industry; indeed, it counted no less than fifty railroads represented by its personnel. If the 711th was to sire the MRS, it needed experience of its own, so in the tepid summer heat of 1941 the unit was shipped down to the cypress swamps of Louisiana to build a railroad to connect Camps Claiborne and Polk, a distance of fifty miles. The C & P ("Crime & Punishment" to the railwaymen who worked it) was completed, including twenty-five bridges, and the final spike pounded in by General Gray, on July 11 (7/11), 1942. Then engines Nos. 7 and 11 (the latter being No. 1, hastily renumbered) touched pilots. It was the 711th's day, as everyone agreed. Among the notables present were Governor S. H. Jones of Louisiana, Kansas City Southern President William Deramus, Sr., and General Matthew B. Ridgway, who sported just one star at the time. Thus the Claiborne & Polk, connecting with the Missouri Pacific at Camp Claiborne and the Kansas City Southern at Camp Polk, was completed. It served the useful purpose of training military railroaders through the war, in addition to their training as active units on their sponsoring roads. The Crime & Punishment was short-lived, its right-of-way long having been returned to the beavers and the cottonmouths, like the old logging railroad whose embankment was utilized over much of the route. The Texas & Pacific 4-6-0's such as No. 7 (*lower right*), shown at the Golden Spike ceremony, and the new War Department 2-8-0's that joined them are now scrap. Even General Carl R. Gray, general director of the MRS (*lower left*), shown driving the last spike, is gone, but the veterans of the C & P still speak fondly of her and recall the Army version of the first rule of railroading, which governed her operations: "Subject to the military situation, safety is of the first importance in the discharge of duty."

Two photos, Col. George M. Welsch, from Larry Lepine

U.S. Army

Moving the Great War Machine

The American participation in World War II was the greatest national war effort in the history of man, and virtually all of it moved by rail, from the mines and oil fields to the processing plants, from subcontractors to assembly plants, from farms and factories to ports of embarkation, from small towns and vast cities to staging areas and air terminals. At Fort Benning, half-tracks (*above*) destined for North Africa were loaded for movement over the Central of Georgia, while light tanks (*below*) were unloaded at a training camp on the Atchison, Topeka and Santa Fe. Although many U.S. servicemen traveled first class (*above right*), others were fed by Army cooks from baggage cars converted into field kitchens, such as the one at Fort Meade, Maryland (*lower right*), in 1941.

AT&SF Railway

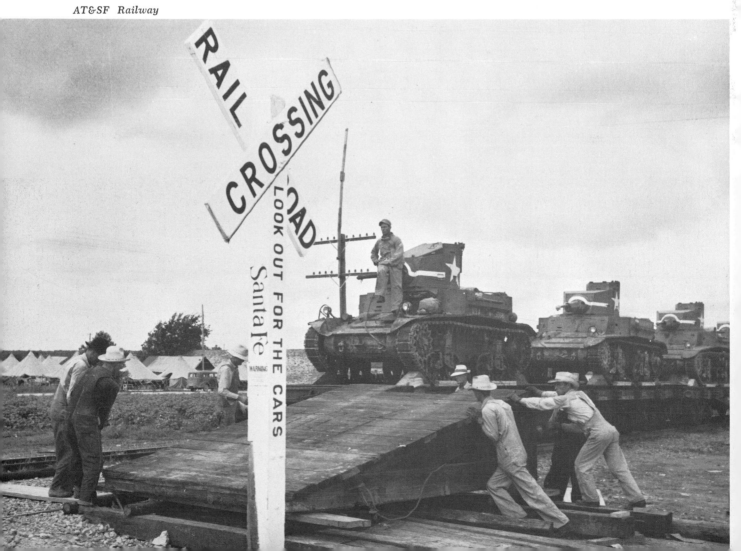

Some soldiers ate in style; for others, Army chow prepared in the baggage car was the rule.

L&N RR

Moving Troops, Civilians, and War Bonds

Each day of the war, the railroads had to move scores of extra trains to meet the needs of the military effort and of the civilians who were restricted from using the highways and the fledgling airlines. On the Louisville & Nashville Railroad in 1942 a troop train ran as "second 99" (*above*)— an extra section of the famed *Pan American*. Pulled by a handsome class J-4 2-8-2, No. 1875, carrying flags for yet another troop extra right behind, the train is southbound just out of Louisville, Kentucky. During the war the L & N more than lived up to its proud nickname, the "Old Reliable." The 46th Company of U.S. Women's Army Corps (WACS) (*below*) is shown forming up before entraining on the Chicago, Burlington & Quincy at Chicago Union Station in 1944. The huge concourse of Union Station in St. Louis (*upper right*) is quiet now; the crowds of military and civilian traffic are no more. The *Texas Special* and the *Sunshine Special* departed for the last time long ago, and the Katy lines are now freight only, with the Frisco and Missouri Pacific offering almost as little in the way of accommodations for passengers. The Burlington promoted the war bond drives by painting coaches red, white, and blue (*lower right*) and lettering them accordingly.

CB&Q RR

Missouri Pacific

Rosie The Riveter

With the acute manpower shortage on the American home front, as in other belligerent nations, millions of women went into war work of all types, including the railroads. Some actually wound up in train service. On the Long Island, they worked as trainmen and were promptly nick-named "Wheels" by the commuters riding to New York. Women worked as ticket agents, tower operators, dispatchers, and in the repair and building shops. They were even found occasionally as brakemen on freights and firemen on oil-burning steam locomotives. In the romantic press of the day the women who went to "war" on the home front were collectively dubbed "Rosie the Riveter." On the CB & Q two genuine "Rosies" (*left*) from the riveting department of that road's Havelock Shops in Nebraska, displayed a new light-weight aluminum hopper car outside sheet. The Union Pacific introduced the world's largest steam locomotive, the 650-ton, 133-foot-long 4-8-8-4 "Big Boy," just prior to the United States entry into the war. A female turntable operator in Wyoming (*below*) is shown as she prepared to turn one of the huge brutes. By 1944 the American Locomotive Company had turned out twenty-five of these locomotives, which UP credited with having averted a serious breakdown in transcontinental war traffic. When the German U-boat submarine offensive reached American shores early in 1942, sinking or driving all of the coastal tankers into ports, the railroads single-handedly supplied the entire industrial eastern seaboard, as well as the Allied fighting forces, with oil. Missouri Pacific 2-8-2 No. 1515 (*right*) by-passed the Little Rock, Arkansas, depot with an auxiliary water tank and a mile-long train of oil cars.

Missouri Pacific

Lend-Lease to the Allies

After much bitter debate among the American people and in Congress, the Lend-Lease Act was passed into law on March 11, 1941, enabling President Franklin D. Roosevelt to supply war material "to be turned over to those nations now in actual war with aggressor nations." Hardly the kind of action to be expected from a neutral power such as the United States claimed to be, Lend-Lease infuriated the Axis leaders and bolstered the waning morale of the British and the captive nations. Even before the Japanese attack brought the United States into active participation in the war, the U.S. Navy and German U-boats were battling in the North Atlantic. Before the end of hostilities, the United States shipped $280 *billion* in war supplies to the Allies—a staggering sum, even in this age of high government spending. These shipments included, among thousands of types of goods, over 20,000 tanks and 25,000 aircraft. The amount of railway equipment was immense. Russia alone received over 1,900 steam and 50 diesel locomotives, plus thousands of tons of other equipment. Among the more interesting items sent to the USSR were at least a dozen mobile steam power plants, to supply electricity to recaptured cities. The first of these (*below*) was turned over to the Soviet government at the American Car and Foundry Company plant in Berwick, Pennsylvania, in 1944.

United Press International

Three photos, Railroad Magazine

CB&Q RR

The Battle of Production

World War II involved all of the greatest industrial nations of the world, but it was not until the manufacturing capacity of the Allies was increased beyond all expectations and the capacity of the Axis dealt devastating aerial bombardment, combined with a loss of their sources of strategic materials, that the eventual victors in this total war could be determined. In the end it was the industrial might of the United States, safe from the ravages of fighting and with its railway network intact, that decided the issue. The erection floor of American Car & Foundry in St. Charles, Missouri (*upper left*), turned out hospital cars for the Army, while especially built Burlington boxcars (*left*) carried fuselage subassemblies for B-17 Flying Fortresses. A sixteen-inch gun (*above*), destined for one of the huge Iowa-class battleships, traveled via the New York, New Haven & Hartford Railroad. In addition to the immense orders for railway equipment, suppliers such as Pullman Standard (*below*) managed to construct thousands of tanks, guns, and other items of heavy military hardware.

With the capitulation of France in June, 1940, the attention of the German high command was turned immediately to England, for Hitler had but two alternatives in achieving total victory in the west: occupation of the British Isles or, failing to achieve invasion, making the British sign an armistice ending hostilities and legitimizing all the German victories of the past five years. As the Germans prepared for Operation Sea Lion—the invasion of England—the British, urged onward by Prime Minister Winston S. Churchill, girded for the battle that was to deny Hitler both alternatives and ultimately to augur the downfall of the Third Reich.

The Battle of Britain was the only major campaign in history to be fought principally in the air, for it was only by wresting aerial superiority away from the Royal Air Force that Göring's *Luftwaffe* could hope to disrupt communications to the extent necessary to isolate a beachhead for the German Army to seize. Once the initial attempt to destroy the RAF was frustrated, with the loss of over 1,700 German aircraft during 17 weeks (July 10–October 31) Göring turned the full fury of the *Luftwaffe* on non-RAF ground targets in an attempt to bring the economy of England to a halt and to demoralize the population. Even at the height of the aerial offensive in late summer of 1940, however, the Germans expended vast amounts of ordnance, aircraft, and experienced crews on the British railway system, failing even once to threaten its vital mission. Foresight on the part of railway officials resulted in alternate lines of telephone communications, stockpiling of such essential parts as switches and standard bridge replacement sections, and contingency plans of operation. All the while, the railways were supplying the vital transport for war. Intermittent bombing of Britain continued through the war, culminating in the V-2 rocket attacks as late as 1945.

The Work of the Luftwaffe

The heaviest raid against a British target occurred the night of November 14, 1940, when five hundred German bombers raided Coventry (*above*), heavily damaging the London Midland and Scottish Railway junction. On April 4, 1942, the crack express train *Night Scotsman* had just arrived at York (*below*) when the *Luftwaffe* paid a visit, leaving little of the wooden coaches except their undercarriages. When the York locomotive shed was hit (*right*), the streamlined A-4 Pacific *Sir Ralph Wedgwood* (ironically named for the chairman of the Railway Executive Committee, charged with wartime emergency planning) became one of only eight British locomotives to be totally destroyed during the war.

The Battle of Britain

Three photos, British Railways

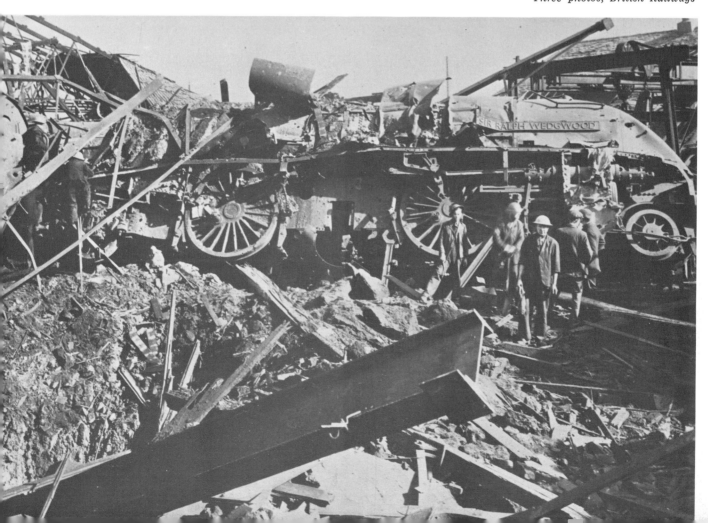

Four photos, British Railways

Preparing for All Eventualities

No sooner had Britain declared war on Germany than the emergency plans went into effect. Fearing an early air war, the authorities arranged for thousands of children to be evacuated from the cities. On October 26, 1939, with the war just eight weeks old and the western front quite silent, trainloads of children (*below*) were being dis-patched to the country from Sheffield, via the LMS Railway. On June 3, 1940, as the last members of the British Expeditionary Force were being evacu-ated from Dunkirk, one of the many British Army units preparing to defend their homeland against invasion (*above*) prepared to entrain at Mill Hill, in the northern London suburbs.

War Production in the Railway Shops

The wartime burdens of any railway shop facility are immense. In addition to keeping increasingly deteriorating equipment operable, these shop complexes must convert existing equipment to specialized wartime uses, such as the former coaches pictured on this page, which emerged from the LMS shops as hospital cars during the first month of the war. Of course, the labor shortage posed major burdens. Unlike most American railways, British rail shops construct their own equipment, including locomotives. This capacity placed such facilities in the category of "heavy industry" and resulted in the various shops' constructing thousands of articles of weaponry.

Newton Abbot, Devon; August 20, 1940

Sunderland Station; September 6, 1940

Whitby Station; September 16, 1940

Whitby Station; October 19, 1940

Prepare, Despair, Repair

The failure of the German aerial offensive to cripple Britain's rail network was indicative of things to come when, four years later, it took over one million tons of bombs to bring the German *Reichsbahn* to a standstill—and this came only after Allied armies were actually swarming into Germany and physically taking possession of the system. All four of the major British railways (Great Western; London, Midland and Scottish; London and North Eastern; Southern) were hit, the Southern suffering heaviest. Before it was over, the combined casualty figures included 395 railwaymen and 498 other persons killed on the railways; 500 locomotives damaged; 637 passenger and 3,321 freight cars destroyed. In addition to ordinary bombs, over 1,000 V-1 robot bombs and a much smaller number of V-2 rockets landed on or close to railway property.

Four photos, British Railways

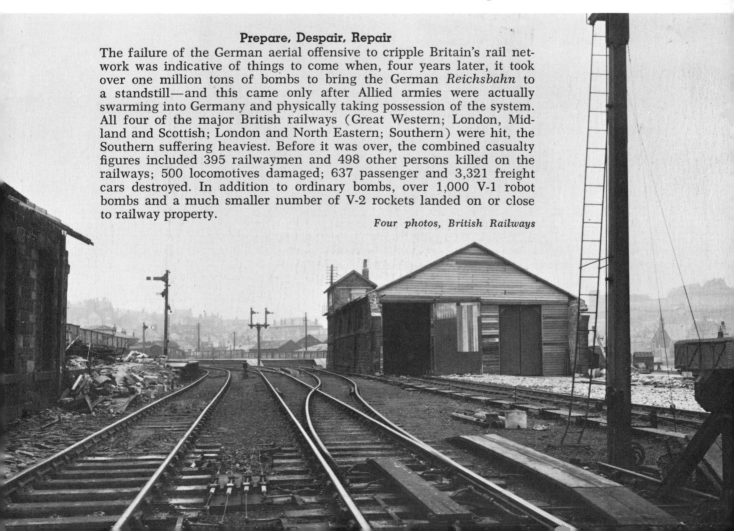

Bristol; December 6, 1940

Four photos, British Railways

Dorset; January 17, 1941

Somerset, September 3, 1942

Paddington Station; March 22, 1944

Turning the Tide of Transport

Stripped of virtually all their heavy equipment, which had to be abandoned on the Continent, the British worked furiously to construct heavy weapons and antiaircraft guns for home defense, while trying to keep their forces east of Gibraltar supplied for the coming African confrontation. As soon as the arsenals, factories, and railway shops could produce the critically needed hardware, such as trucks and Bren Gun Carriers (*above*) being unloaded at Banbury, and tanks (*below*), they were rushed to defend the Channel coast. An armored unit rolled through Berkhamsted (*right*) while as far away as Stranraer, in Scotland, a Southern Railway car ferry, on loan to the LMS (*lower right*), was armor-plated and saw service ferrying supplies to RAF bases in Northern Ireland. As an example of the railway industry's incredible potential for expansion, the LMS shops alone built hundreds of tanks, four thousand pairs of airplane wings, armor-plated hundreds of merchant's trucks for defense against invasion

the famous "Armadillos"—as well as such varied items as twenty-seven thousand 1/1000-inch tolerance gunsights, eight thousand assault boats, millions of ammunition shell casings, and special cars to transport priceless treasures from the National Art Gallery to safe storage!

Four photos, British Railways

The Man of the Century

Sir Winston Churchill, the wartime Prime Minister whom the unappreciative British electorate dismissed immediately after he had led them from the verge of total defeat, through "their finest hour" to ultimate triumph, is shown (*above*) with Lady Churchill and various aides after returning to London by train on August 23, 1941. The worst dangers immediately behind them, Churchill and the English people had good cause for optimism; eleven days earlier, on board HMS *Prince of Wales* off the coast of Newfoundland, the Prime Minister and President Franklin D. Roosevelt had issued the Atlantic Charter. This document, containing a phrase referring to "the final destruction of the Nazi tyrrany," virtually assured the world that the time of American entry into the war was close at hand. Although poison gas was never used even in the most desperate moments of World War II, on a date such as May 21, 1940, a Great Western engine driver (*left*) had no idea of what to expect and was consequently prepared, with mask and helmet, for any eventuality.

British Railways

War on the Home Front

With a new airborne threat in the form of pilotless missiles rising up from across the channel, Great Western telephone operators (*above*) carried on their communications from beneath their desks on October 6, 1944. Although little has been written on the subject, apparently there were some prisoner exchanges during the war. On October 14, 1943, a group of German military prisoners (*below*) disembarked from a train pulled by the appropriately named LMS locomotive *Revenge* in Glasgow, Scotland. Under armed escort they boarded the Red Cross ship *Atlantis* for the voyage back to Germany.

U.S. Army

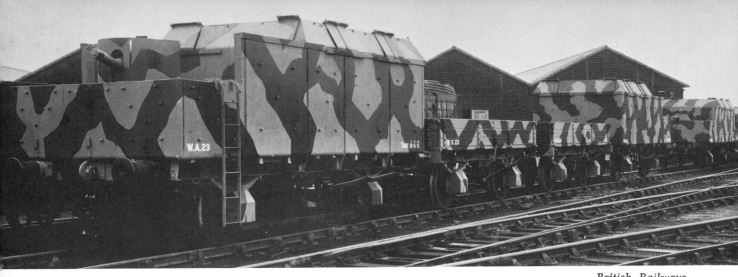

British Railways
Imperial War Museum

UPI

Standard and Narrow-Gauge Armored Trains

One of the vital elements of the coastal defense of England was built around lightly armored trains, such as the gun car and tender teams (*above left*) outshopped by the LMS Derby Works on July 5, 1940. They were coupled in pairs, fore and aft of a locomotive (*left*), and operated extensively for the duration of the invasion threat. The troops in this particular gun crew are exiled Polish soldiers, doing what they can in the effort against the occupiers of their homeland. Coincidentally, this gun car, No. WA 23, is the same one in the lead of the lineup in the photograph above, which was taken seven months later, on February 4, 1941. On this page are two photographs indicative of the paradox of war. There is, on the southeast coast of England, a light railway renowned the world over as being the narrowest-gauge common carrier in existence, the Romney, Hythe and Dymchurch Railway. Built for the most peaceful of purposes —to serve the beach resort areas of Kent—the RHD found itself right in the midst of the expected beachhead of Operation Sea Lion. Consequently, the British Army took over its operation, including the armor-plating of one of its locomotives and installation of machine guns and anti-tank rifles. To add to its fame, the RHD possessed what was undoubtedly the most diminutive armored train in the world. It managed to see lots of action, being a frequent target of the *Luftwaffe*. The thousands of British Tommies who rode behind double-headed power from Dungeness Point to Hythe for weekend revelry, however, ultimately did more damage than Göring's marauders. In the Romney, Hythe and Dymchurch was symbolized the complete mobilization of a people determined to survive as a nation against incredible odds. The RHD—and the rest of England—made it!

Imperial War Museum

Four Thousand Miles of Sand

Indian Ministry of Defence

The coming of war in Europe created a succession of weird situations in the arid regions of North Africa, the Arabian peninsula, and southwest Asia. In the Italian colonies of Libya and Italian Somaliland the Axis powers possessed vast territory and bases in Africa. The Italian attack on Ethiopia in 1935 was one of the salient preludes to the European conflict and proved the impotence of the League of Nations. After the fall of France in June, 1940, the French North African colonies of Morocco, Algeria, and Tunisia (the latter two bordering on Libya) assumed great importance. Although their military commanders supported the Nazi-imposed French Vichy government at home, the loyalties of many officers leaned toward the Allied cause. Hitler's comparatively benign treatment of conquered France irked his Italian allies, who always felt that the Germans grossly underrated the importance of the Mediterranean. The wide latitude of action accorded the French commanders in Africa by the Germans also tended to stifle Italian designs on French territory—a circumstance of Hitler's planning which was very deliberate.

Far from ordering the French around in Africa, the Germans often had to carry out delicate negotiations to assure protection of their vulnerable western flank, as General Erwin Rommel's *Afrika Korps* swept toward the Suez Canal and the Arabian oil fields. In the twisted politics of May, 1941, the French command wrangled permission to rearm its African colonial forces against a possible British attack, granting the German Army in return the right to use the strategic Bizerte-Gabes railway in Tunisia! There were other French concessions, including the granting of railway rights to the Axis through Syria, in support of the drive on the Arabian oil fields and Suez. When the Anglo-American invasion of North Africa material-

ized in 1942, some French units offered brief—although at times tough—resistance to their "liberators." Most of it was half-hearted, and the French forces either surrendered or joined the Allies. As the Allied armies moved east and west to trap the Axis army in Tunisia, much railway activity was required to support their rapid advances.

Further east, British Empire forces, including Indian, Australian, and New Zealand railway units, took over the construction and operation of railways in Egypt and Iraq, while American and British railway battalions performed one of the greatest transportation successes of the war: supplying the Russian armies of the Caucasus front from Persian Gulf ports via the operationally hazardous and dangerously rugged terrain traversed by 866 miles of the Iranian State Railways from the Persian Gulf to Teheran.

Supplying the Desert Armies

As Mussolini's expeditionary forces drove into Kenya and the Anglo-Egyptian Sudan, the railhead of Kassala became a vital forward supply area. In March, 1941, as the British Army on the Nile pushed the Italians back through Ethiopia, Indian troops (*above*) unloaded petrol cans at Kassala station, in the Sudan. That same month, German General Erwin Rommel arrived in Libya and, on the twenty-fourth, began his spectacular career as the "Desert Fox" by launching his long drive on Egypt. Once again Hitler had to rush troops into a void left by Mussolini's ambitious incompetence. With the attack on Russia just three months off, the Germans could ill afford to send equipment such as the desert-camouflaged trucks (*upper right*) shown in Treuchtlingen, Germany, en route to Rommel. Australian troops for General Bernard Montgomery's Eighth Army are shown detraining (*right*) during a sandstorm on the African desert.

Crossing the Western Desert

As Rommel launched his offensive on Alamein, the British Empire forces worked furiously westward across the Egyptian desert to meet the threat—by rail. Constructed largely by Indian and New Zealand railway troops, the Western Desert line was completed just in time to rush tens of thousands of tons of supplies and thousands of troops from the port facilities at Suez to the static front at Alamein in the summer of 1942. On October 23, with the railway supplying the necessary logistics, General Montgomery launched the attack that, seven months later, resulted in the annihilation of the *Afrika Korps.* These photos show the Indians and New Zealanders constructing the Western Desert line, using rails rolled in India, in March, 1942.

All photos, Indian Ministry of Defence

108

Australian War Memorial

Beyond Alamein

Only two weeks after Montgomery attacked Rommel at Alamein, the first train (*upper left*) arrived at Alamein station, followed by an Egyptian State Railways steel caboose, on November 6, 1942. In June, 1942, sappers of an Australian engineer unit (*above*) used an American-built Lima crane to assemble a deckspan bridge south of Byblos (now Jubail), Lebanon. Indian troops (*right*) are shown leaving Haifa, Palestine, for Egypt in November, 1944. When the United States sent dozens of Whitcomb diesels to Egypt to supplement the British steam locomotives (the operation of which was greatly hampered by the scarcity of water), the U.S. Army 760th Railway Shop Battalion (Diesel) was sent along to maintain them. One of the diesels, painted white to reflect heat, left the 760th yard at Simila, Egypt (*lower left*), on July 2, 1943. Duty on the Simila rail line was rough, and an anonymous member of the 760th summed up the feelings of his fellow Army railroaders:

Out on the wind swept desert
    Camp Simila is the spot
Battling the terrible dust storms
    In the land that God forgot.

Out with the Wogs and Bedouins,
    Out where the boys get blue,
Out in the wind-swept desert
    Six thousand miles from you.

At night the wind keeps blowing
    More than we can stand,
Penned in like convicts
    But defenders of our land.

We are the boys of the 760th
    Earning our meager pay
Guarding folks with millions
    For a buck and a half a day.

No one cares if we are living
    No one gives a damn
And we are soon forgotten,
    We're just Lend-Leased by Uncle Sam.

Only three years we can stand it
    Three years of our life we'll miss.
Boys, don't let the Draft Board get you
    And for God's sake don't enlist.

We are soldiers so they tell us
    But we hear no bands of brass
But some day we'll get Hitler
    And shove Egypt up his ——.

Indian Ministry of Defence

Battle for the Oilfields

The rich oilfields of Iraq, Iran, and Arabia are the main source of fuel for European industry and transport. At the onset of World War II both British and German strategists were acutely aware of this fact and compensated for it in all of their planning. By 1941 the German Army was engaged in a giant pincers movement that straddled the Mediterranean and was poised to clamp shut on the Suez Canal and the Iraqi oil fields. As Rommel thrust into Egypt, the German campaign in the Balkans overcame Greece, seized Crete, and moved into Vichy Syria. By late summer, German forces in Russia threatened the oil fields from the north. Since British strength was concentrated in Egypt and Vichy Syria was a weak outpost on Iraq's western flank, British Commonwealth forces moved into Syria, deliberately advancing along and securing the railways, which had been cut by sabotage and *Luftwaffe* air strikes. In July, 1941, after Commonwealth forces had advanced on Baghdad by rail, the Vichy government of Syria collapsed, along with the immediate threat of a German take-over of the oilfields. The photos on these pages show railway soldiers of the Indian Army operating Indian locomotives in Iraq in 1942. During the 1941–42 period, the Vichy French controlled the Trans-Sahara Railway in Northwest Africa. When the French arrested hundreds of their countrymen in Africa for treason, they were sent, along with many Foreign Legionnaires of nationalities whose countries were at war with Germany, to work on the Trans-Sahara Railway. There, hundreds of miles from scrutiny by even his own superiors in the *Wehrmacht*, the German railway commander allowed the prisoners to be flogged, beaten, starved, and worked to death by the sadistic guards in the torrid heat of day and the icy winds of the nighttime desert.

Four photos, Indian Ministry of Defence

U.S. Military Railwaymen Enter the War

It was ironic that on the night of November 8, 1942, less than twenty-four hours after Allied forces stormed the North African coast in the first assault on Axis-occupied territory, Hitler made far-reaching military and political decisions using a map torn out of a railway guide. He had arrived in Munich to formulate new policies toward France in light of the invasion of the latter's vast African colonial empire, and the map from a guide in his headquarters railway car was the handiest chart available. Meanwhile, in the railroad yard in St. Leu, Algeria, two American soldiers of the 591st Engineer Boat Regiment had good reason to grin (*above*) on the first day of the invasion. They are guarding a meter-gauge French car loaded with casks of vintage wine. Operation Torch, the assault on Rommel's rear, quickly grew into a war of logistics, just as Montgomery's forces were beginning to utilize the advantages of the Western Desert Railway in Egypt. The original plans called for as many as 19 U.S. Army Railway Operating Battalions to operate the French railways in North

Africa, plus supporting units, shop battalions, and headquarters units, not to mention an almost equal number of British outfits. A combination of efficiency under combat conditions and the utilization of French and Arab railwaymen cut these requirements by almost two-thirds in actual practice. Although the native railwaymen were often reluctant to work for the invaders, the sharp "clank" of a carbine bolt cocked in the hands of an American soldier-trainman overcame language and attitude barriers. It was here that the doctrines of the MRS were tested, revised, and forged into the operating practices that were to amaze friend and foe alike, as the American railroaders went on to carry the freight of victory even to Germany itself, just two years later. Ultimately the MRS would acquire and operate old and new, American and foreign, excellent and wrecked equipment in six different gauges to operate in six major campaigns of World War II. On February 17, 1943, when a Signal Corps photographer took photos of the 727th ROB operating in Tebessa, Algeria (*right*), the unit's commander, Lieutenant Colonel

Fred W. Okie, and several of his officers and men had been reported missing in action for three days. The final German offensive, at Kasserine Pass, was spilling deep into 727th territory. Okie had taken five trains to Gafsa, to evacuate the city before the onslaught of a *Panzer* corps. He succeeded, but south of Thelepte a major disaster had occurred when U.S. Army Engineers, not realizing that Okie's trains were, in this situation of rapidly moving desert warfare, already *between* the German and Allied lines, blew up a large viaduct shortly before the arrival of the last four trains. Okie was not with these trains, having raced out of Metlaoui by truck mere yards ahead of the German tanks that took the town. The trains at the wrecked bridge were backed up, and one trainload of precious ammunition was hidden in a tunnel, safe from the *Luftwaffe*. After readying the other trains for demolition, the men of the 727th, perhaps already behind the German front, hid the loco-

motives in phosphate mines, stripped them of their irreplaceable side rods and valve motion, loaded the parts in a two-and-a-half-ton truck, and struck out from Moulares. They too got out after being spotted by German armor. Approaching the Allied lines, the men of the 727th were fired upon by Senegalese troops who thought they were Germans. On the night of February 15, a crew of the 727th that had managed to infiltrate back through the German lines brought out the ammunition train in spite of the failure of an old French engine and got it to the wrecked bridge where the cargo was transferred to trucks. All of the officers and men of the 727th who had been reported as killed or missing in the battle for Kasserine Pass, the worst Allied defeat of the North African campaign, made it back to their lines by February 17, after performing their duties in a manner that would have brought credit to even the most experienced combat troops.

Three photos, U.S. Army

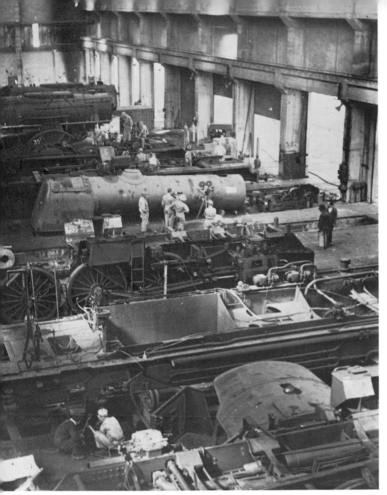

The 1400-Mile Desert Supply Line

Hostilities in North Africa ended on May 12, 1943 —six months after the 761st Railway Transportation Company, the first MRS unit to arrive in a combat zone, landed at Oran to take over switching duties in that strategic port. By the time the *Afrika Korps* was defeated, entire shiploads of American railway troops, locomotives, cars, rails, and dozens of other items of railway supply were arriving almost daily. Much of this equipment, including standard U.S. 2-8-0 No. 1779, was unloaded in Casablanca, French Morocco (*below*), and in Oran, Algeria. In spite of the decrepit condition of the French railways, which was due to three years of wartime-deferred maintenance, added to decades of colonial neglect, there were some pleasant surprises for the MRS, such as a very modern and intact locomotive shop (*left*) and large quantities of railway supplies that the Axis forces had had no time to destroy. During the six months following Torch over eleven million tons of supplies were landed to support the Allies, most of it leaving the ports by rail. The MRS had no time to let up on the momentum they had established during the campaign, and a continuous flood of troops, military supplies, railway equipment, and MRS units moved ever eastward along the 1,400 miles of rail between Casablanca and Tunis, in a massive buildup for the invasion of Sicily—less than two months after the end of the African fighting.

Two photos, U.S. Army from Railroad Magazine

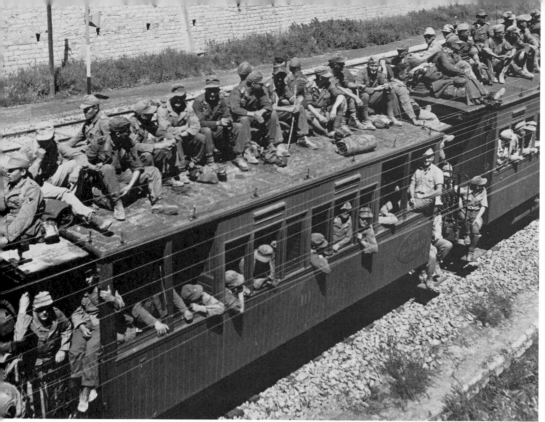

Winding up the African Campaign

British railway units in Africa brought with them such War Department locomotives as No. 167 (*below*), a Great Western–designed 0-6-0. On February 25, 1943, English railway soldiers (*upper right*) operated a six-wheel tank shunter on her trial run in Tripoli. A trainload of Germans passed through Tunis (*upper left*) on the way to POW camps on the day of the final surrender, May 12, 1943. After this date, the Allied railwaymen no longer had to dodge the *Luftwaffe* and exchange fire with saboteurs, but they still had to contend with Arab brakemen who fell asleep on the job, causing runaways that sometimes resulted in fatal wrecks. They still were exhausted after twenty-hour runs in 130° desert heat. They were still risking death by asphyxiation in tunnels. Steam locomotive boilers still frothed and foamed and broke down because of impure water. Mines and booby traps still made a walk of a few feet

from the right-of-way very risky in many areas. In spite of these hazards, every impossible task handed to the railway troops was accomplished—usually ahead of schedule—including the return of the rehabilitated system to French control by the end of 1943, as the MRS units and headquarters moved up to Italy. Supreme Allied Commander General Dwight D. Eisenhower fully realized the importance of his railway units, as he acknowledged in *Crusade in Europe:* ". . . our Military Railway Service engineers were working miracles in improving the decrepit French line leading to the front. When we went into North Africa the railway could daily deliver a maximum of 900 tons of supplies. By introducing Yankee energy and modern American methods of operation the Military Railway Service increased the daily tonnage to 3,000 and this before they received a single extra engine or boxcar from the United States."

Three photos, Imperial War Museum

Railroad Magazine

The Back Door to Russia

By mid-1941, German spearheads of the *Afrika Korps* were nearing the Egyptian border, and on the newly opened eastern front, Army Group South was advancing rapidly through the Ukraine toward the Caucasus mountains and the Caspian Sea. Beyond lay the ultimate objective: the oil fields of Iran and the closing of the pincers on Suez. It was also realized that Anglo-American Lend-Lease supplies to Russia would be very limited if they had to travel via the U-boat- and *Luftwaffe*-controlled sea routes to Murmansk and Archangel, which were icebound during the long Russian winters. This left the British and Russians with but one alternative: the priceless Trans-Iranian Railway. Operationally it was one of the most brutal stretches of track in the world, traversing hundreds of miles of desert where station thermometers gave readings in the 140's (Fahrenheit), locomotive water was almost nonexistent, and sand a constant enemy. Beyond the desert the railway is considered one of the engineering marvels of the world, as it assaults the mountains in which Teheran is nestled between the oil-soaked sands and the Caspian Sea. Here the steep grades, hairpin curves, subzero temperatures, 231 tunnels, and 4,201 bridges (the vast majority of which are in the north) made peacetime railroading a most dangerous undertaking. World War II on the Iranian Railway, with its huge increase in traffic, proved once again that there are virtually no limits to the expansion of an existing and in-service rail line; this capability is far beyond anything ever imagined for any other type of transport. On August 25, 1941, Russian troops occupied northern Iran and Red Army railway units took over the operation of the lines leading east and west out of Teheran up to Russia on both coasts of the Cas-

pian Sea. At the same time, the British took over the 866 miles of line from the Persian Gulf port of Bandar Shahpur to Teheran. Bandar Shahpur could only handle two ocean vessels at once, so the Royal Engineers began a crash program of expanding the port facilities, while extending two branch lines to two new ports: Khorramshar and Tanuma. The prewar tonnage carried by the Iranian State Railway amounted to about two hundred tons a day, hardly two-thirds of the requirements of one Russian division. South of Stalingrad the Russian Army of the Caucasus fielded upward of thirty divisions. A major portion of their supplies—four million tons by V-E Day—had to come via the Iranian Railway. That four million tons delivered to Russia over the Trans-Iranian line meant a daily increase of an average of *twenty times* the prewar level. On peak days the traffic moved was thirty times greater. All this was accomplished without double-tracking the line, a feat which would have taken years to complete. By the time the U.S. Army took over the operation of the line south of Teheran from the British early in 1943, the Royal Engineers had built over forty passing sidings and hundreds of track miles of storage and marshalling yards. To supplement the existing Iranian roster of fewer than one hundred steam locomotives (two-thirds of them German-built) the British brought in fifty-four steamers. At the Cairo Conference in 1942 President Roosevelt, after top-secret discussions with Prime Minister Churchill on the subject, ordered Ambassador W. Averill Harriman, a man of wide railroad experience, to arrange for the MRS to take over the delivery of American Lend-Lease supplies via the IRS. Ultimately the Americans brought in ninety-two new 2-8-2 locomotives, such as the trim Lima product (*above*) and sixty-seven 1,000-horsepower Alco diesels. Although steam outnumbered the diesels more than four to one in Iran, the Alcos received much publicity, because they were among the first diesels to be extensively deployed in the war and because of their definite advantages over steam in the waterless desert. Many of the imported locomotives were unloaded into barges at Khorramshar and sent up the Karun River to Ahwaz (*upper right*), where the entire electric supply in the town was cut off to supply power to the giant cranes that unloaded engines such as this British 2-8-0 on June 7, 1942. At Camp Atterbury, named for the Director-General of the MRS in World

Imperial War Museum

War I, the U.S. Army railway terminal in Teheran (*lower right*) housed both American and British War Department motive power on January 8, 1945. As in most campaigns, the GI railroaders in Iran were usually overworked far beyond the limits of the "sixteen-hour law" that governs American civilian rail operations. The resulting fatigue caused many an engine man to fall asleep in the cab. When engineer Carl Lopez of the 791st Railway Operating Battalion returned to duty after two weeks' hospitalization, he took out a diesel train on a run from Andimeshk to Do Roud. Lopez' fireman, also worked beyond endurance, fell asleep at about the same time as Lopez. One of the diesel units stalled out, but the other, although at a dead stop, continued spinning its wheels. The resulting rail "burns" (*left*) were considered by most railroaders to be among the worst on record. Even if a rail line can be worked far beyond its capacity in wartime, there is still the limitation of human endurance to be considered. It is interesting to note that the Iranian State Railway MRS timetable for October 30, 1944, quotes the cardinal rule of railroading: ". . . safety is of first importance in the discharge of duty." This phrase, however, was preceded in all MRS World War II timetables by the following qualification: "Subject to the military situation. . . ."

U.S. Army

Three photos, U.S. Army

British Railways

Troublesome Allies

Since the Western powers and the Soviet Union were, to word it mildly, hardly ideally suited ideologically to be allies (a fact that thoroughly confused the Nazis, who were never reconciled to having the "plutocrats and the bolsheviks" aligned against them), the distrust and overt hostility between the two systems, which was neatly buried under an avalanche of propaganda in 1941, occasionally surfaced. It nearly erupted in Iran in 1943, but the Persian Gulf Service Command (PGSC) was fairly remote and not actually a combat area, so the magnitude of the situation never did reach the home front. A root of the problem was that the American technology and productive capacity, which was sinking the enemies of the United States, was swamping the Russians in the process. They just could not unload the trains as fast as the 711th, 730th, and 791st ROB's were delivering them. The result was chaotic, as hundreds of cars filled the Teheran storage yards (*upper left*) waiting to be transferred to the Russians. Had the Russians been cooperative, the operation may have been closer to schedule, but they often refused to accept whole trainloads, demanding that the 730th crews switch out certain cars and move them exactly where the Russians wanted them. The Russians then devised a quaint method of solving the problem of too many cars to unload: they simply floated many of the cars across the Caspian Sea and never returned them. By 1943, the turn-around time for loaded tank cars leaving the Persian Gulf and returning from Russian depots was thirty days, instead of the ample allotment of fifteen. The ultimate result was that by the first week in August, 1943, virtually the entire fleet of about five thousand serviceable freight cars was up at the north end of the line waiting to be unloaded! In desperation the MRS clamped a six-day embargo on shipments to Russia, during which time no Lend-Lease freight was loaded at the ports and nothing was sent to the Russians in Teheran. The

situation soon improved. The standard British 2-8-0's, such as the one on an unidentified Iranian turntable (*middle left*), were fitted with horizontal bar pilots. On February 2, 1943, two other English "W-D's" met head-on (*lower left*) during the transition period from British to America operation. Officers of both countries inspected the wreck, which occurred between Khorramshar and Ahwaz. In 1942 three British 2-8-0's, christened "Churchill's Reply" (*above*), awaited clearance to move freight to Russia from Ahwaz. One of the original Iranian State Railways port switch engines (*right*) is pictured shunting loads of Lend-Lease. The little tank engine, like most of Iran's motive power, was built in Germany after the Shah began construction of the ISR in 1927. These German locomotives ironically played a major role in bringing about the defeat of their homeland.

Photoworld

Railroad Magazine

Vicissitudes of Operating the Iranian Railway

Of all the military railway lines in World War II, the Trans-Iranian was one of the most difficult to operate. The only thing missing was battle damage, although there was much sabotage from a very large pro-German segment of the native population. All of those cuts, fills, bridges, and tunnels were very easily sabotaged, so tough Indian troops guarded the line. Heavily armed bandits attacked trains and lonely stations, so the Allied troops, including MRS personnel, operated under semicombat conditions. When the train crews finally got through the heat, the tunnels, the firefights with bandits, sabotage, wrecks, loneliness, and privation, they often had to take insults from the Russians, although there was some camaraderie (*upper left*) between the MRS crews and Russian guards in Teheran and the Soviet government, in a rare show of appreciation, awarded medals to some MRS officers and men. American and Iranian railroad men (*lower left*) worked together in the Persian Gulf Command. The heat was so intense that the Alco diesels (*above right*) operated with the engine access doors removed, in spite of the increased danger of sand damage. Locomotives used so much sand on the grades that crewmen frequently had to run ahead with buckets of sand and throw it on the rails by hand. Runaways were a continuous problem. Once, during such an unnerving incident, an Arab brakeman was loudly beseeching Allah for deliverance. "Pinky" Powers, an MRS conductor, gave up on the brakes, pushed the Arab aside, and reportedly said, "Move over and let a good Catholic show you how to pray!" Meanwhile, Captain W. Thomas Rice arrived to take command of a detachment of the 711th at Khorramshar. The yardmaster's office was in the charge of William T. Church when a sergeant brought in several cases of beer destined for the officer's mess, which had fallen out of a car during switching. Church locked up the precious foam while the sergeant went out to locate the car from which it came. Soon Captain Rice and the military police commander arrived, searching for the beer, convinced that it had been stolen. When the MP major inquired about the contents of the sealed locker behind a desk, Church knew that he could never explain the beer stashed in it. Church said that it contained supplies. When asked who had

the key, Church admitted that he did. Just then, Rice turned, ushered the MP officer out the door, and bid Church a good evening. Church was visibly shaken, and he still wonders if Rice knew what was in the locker! The beer was returned to the car, Church has become quite a railway historian since the war, and Rice went on to become superintendent of the IRS Central Division (791st ROB) and later a major general and one of America's leading railroad officials. His beer-spotting ability, however, is still a mystery. For many a lonely MRS detachment maintaining the block stations of the Iranian Railway, the American Red Cross Trainmobile, shown at Sepid Dashte (*below*), was the only diversion from the boredom and dangers of their existence. Along with Captain Stanley E. Smith, the "Caboose Chaplain" of the MRS in Iran, these Red Cross volunteers brought entertainment, comfort, books, friendly talk, and a touch of home to the weary railroad soldiers who worked so hard and accomplished so much on the barren plains and mountain passes of Iran.

American Red Cross

Across the Mediterranean and up the Boot

With the defeat of Rommel's *Afrika Korps*, the Allies struck northward across the Mediterranean and into the "soft underbelly" of the Axis. Only two days after the Allied troops assaulted the island of Sicily, on July 10, 1943, an advance party of the 727th Railway Operating Battalion led by that unit's commander, Colonel Fred W. Okie, came ashore on the U.S. Seventh Army beachhead at Licata. They immediately fired up a locomotive, ran a reconnaissance to the front at Campobello, fifteen miles northward, made quick repairs, and began supplying the 3rd Division the same day! So, only forty-eight hours after D-day, 400 tons moved to the front by rail. On July 13, 600 tons were carried; on July 14, 800 tons; and the spiral continued upward, until by August 30 approximately 170,000 tons had been handled in military freight alone. The average of 3,400 tons daily did not include the civilian passenger and freight traffic, troop trains, and prisoners-of-war trains. The mountainous terrain of Sicily rendered the road network nearly useless for long-distance truck hauls, which were Seventh Army Commander General George S. Patton's favorite means of transport. The 727th repaired track and equipment, rebuilt wrecked bridges, and cleared tunnel cave-ins so rapidly that rail supply of front-line troops was continuous and proved a major factor in cutting down the timetable for the capture of Sicily from eighty-five to just thirty-eight days. So excellent was the performance of the 727th that Patton, a man not lavish in bestowing praise, issued a commendation that reflected the appreciation and awe the combat forces felt for the efforts of the railroad troops. It read, in part: " . . . made

a reconnaissance of the railroad yards, organized native rail workers, located equipment, had steam up, and made a reconnaissance of the rail lines within four hours after landing. . . ."

Sicily became the staging area for the Italian campaign even before Axis resistance was crushed, and on September 3, 1943, two divisions of the British Eighth Army crossed the Strait of Messina and gained a toehold on the toe of the Italian boot. There followed twenty months of brutal ground and aerial combat, which often saw the facilities of the Italian State Railways as primary objectives.

Destroying and Rebuilding the Yards

The dual-gauge yard at Canicatti, Sicily (*below*), shown after track restoration by the 727th ROB. The Allied forces were fortunate to capture over 300 locomotives and 3,500 freight cars in good condition, which were immediately pressed into service. Much of this material was of brand-new German manufacture, including storehouses of supplies and a considerable amount of the famous Roth Wagner standard prefabricated bridge units. On balance, however, there was much sabotage by local fascists and acute locomotive water shortages early in the campaign. As one locomotive was receiving five thousand gallons of water by hose from a warship, a flight of German aircraft leisurely strafed the operation. The Navy and the MRS men calmly completed the watering chore, then both steamed on their respective courses, undaunted and undamaged by the attack! During Operation Strangle, the great aerial offensive of 1944 that attempted to sever all rail ties between Italy and Germany, a B-26 of the 1st Tactical Air Force (*left*) is shown pulling up from a run over the German-held Florence railway yards.

The Rails of "Il Duce"

Whenever the achievements of Benito Mussolini, the premier of Italy during its Fascist era, are discussed, it is invariably pointed out that he made the trains run on time. In fact, during the 1930's the Italian State Railways became one of the finest, most modern rail networks in the world. Vast stretches, especially in the mountainous north, were electrified, track and structures were upgraded, and modern steam power and cars were built. In the early 1940's German technology added even more improvements. Indeed the entire Italian wartime economy rode the rails, as is evident by the fact that virtually all of her coal, which before the war had come from Germany by barge, was shipped over the Alps by rail. Italian industries required one million tons of coal a month to operate, and by early 1942 the Germans were able to send only about half that amount, cutting war production accordingly. The first reversals for the Axis were felt on the rail links between the two principal powers. Less than a month after the initial landings on the Italian peninsula, the U.S. Fifth Army captured Naples. Several of the little Italian six-wheel tank switchers in Naples were named for prominent American generals of the Italian front (*left*) in November, 1943. The following month, antiaircraft guns mounted by American soldiers on gondola cars (*lower right*) fired at German planes. Camouflaged German aircraft parts were still resting on wrecked flatcars in the background. When the retreating Germans failed in their attempt to blow up Mussolini's armored command car in a tunnel, U.S. troops captured the car, cut the roof off, and mounted antiaircraft batteries on it. The car, originally a cherished gift to *Il Duce* from Hitler, is shown in its new role (*right*) at the depot in Caserta, twenty miles north of Naples.

Railroad Magazine

Three photos, U.S. Army

Bundesarchiv

National Archives

German "Trackwolf"

Probably the most ingenious piece of railway equipment used during the Second World War was devised by German Army Engineers when it was realized that the seemingly invincible *Wehrmacht* had seen a serious altering of the fortunes of battle. Having quickly repaired damaged trackage in the occupied countries themselves, the Germans sought more effective methods of covering withdrawals by rail than those previously used. All the switch frogs or points could be blown, but were rapidly replaced. Even destroyed bridges and dynamited tunnels could be rebuilt in relatively short spans of time; certainly soon enough to keep up with the advancing army in all but the most effective *Blitzkrieg*. Perhaps learning a lesson from General W. T. Sherman, who obliterated the railroads of central Georgia during the American Civil War eighty years earlier, the Germans decided that the only way to militarily disrupt a rail line was to totally destroy it. That meant tearing up the ties and breaking the rails. The solution came in the form of a gigantic hook, called a "track wolf" by the Germans. When there was time for an orderly phased withdrawal, the "scarifier" or track-ripper, as it was known to American railroaders, was employed with devastating success. Usually pulled by three or four locomotives, the adjustable hook would be dropped onto the center of the track, where it snapped wood or con-

crete ties in half and bent steel ties into scrap. It usually bent and kinked the rails and, in the process, dug several feet into the subsurface, churning and mixing up cinders, ballast and earthwork. Construction of the "scarifiers" varied in design details (variations are seen in this volume's chapters on France and Russia), but the most sophisticated design was exemplified in the specimen that operated in Italy (*right*) in 1944. To ensure the destruction of the rails, two chutes delivered magnetic delayed-action explosive charges, which automatically blew the center of each rail. In this extremely rare and poorly reproduced photograph, the troops operating the track wolf are shown utilizing the charges. One charge had moved down the left chute almost to the bottom. It was nearly hidden by the protective shield that prevented the charges from bouncing out, for the "scarifier" was extremely rough-riding. The soldier seated in the left foreground reached for another charge held by the man behind. The operator of the other chute held a charge, preparatory to dropping it down the slide, while the man to the rear passed more explosives forward. This device could completely destroy several miles of track an hour. German tankmen (*above*) camouflaged their vehicle, which was captured from the French four years earlier, as they prepared to retreat by rail before the Allied advance up the Italian peninsula in 1944.

The 713th and 727th—Comrades in Arms and Rails

From North Africa to Germany the 713th and 727th Railway Operating
Battalions had four major assignments in common and always in adjoining and overlapping territory. The only exception was the side trip to
Sicily of the 727th, which was bypassed by the 713th on its assault from
Tunisia to Naples. As the U.S. Fifth Army advanced from Naples to Rome
and on to Terni, the 713th ROB was right behind and sometimes right up
with the front-line forces. So close to the front was the 713th operating, in
fact, that it became tongue-in-cheek practice to warn conductors against
turning their trains over to German yardmasters. By July, 1944, just a
month after the capture of Rome, the 727th was far to the northwest,
once again rehabilitating the tracks right behind the Fifth Army front
and under constant bombing and strafing by the *Luftwaffe*. A trainload of
Sherman tanks (*above*) is shown crossing a bridge on the line between
Orbatello and Grosseto, which had been thoroughly demolished by Allied
air power and quickly replaced by the 727th and the Army Engineers. By
July 20 service had been restored in the savagely disputed and totally
demolished town of Cassino. Two diesels, veterans of the North African
campaign, were photographed bringing the first train from Naples to
Rome past the rubble of the depot (*right*) and within the shadows of the
remnants of the famous Abbey of Monte Cassino, which was destroyed by
Allied air power five months earlier. Because of the acute coal shortage
in Italy, the Whitcomb diesel engines, along with the 760th Railway Shop
Battalion (Diesel), had been rushed up from the Middle East, where they
successfully filled in until the arrival of coal for steam power and the rebuilding of electrified lines. After the 715th ROB took over Cassino, they
set up a telegraph station in a caboose (*upper right*). One day Lieutenant
A. W. Arnell, the general yardmaster, got no answer when he tried to raise
the operator (one of the men in the photo). Upon investigating, Arnell found
the man down on the bank of the Rapido River, where he had snagged the
body of a dead German officer and removed his belt, complete with a
brand-new automatic pistol. He then shoved the body back out into the
river, received a dressing-down from Arnell, and returned to his post to
relay the messages of the MRS and to clean his war souvenir. Meanwhile the 761st Railway Transportation Company had arrived in Naples
from Oran in June to take over switching duties in the bustling port.
Charlie "Doc" Russell was the Naples general yardmaster. One day he told
a few of his more conscientious men to watch for high boxcars, which were
needed to transport the camels of a French colonial unit due in the area
shortly. The men scurried out, leaving "Doc" to chuckle at his practical
joke. The tables were turned when his CO told him to hold high-sided
cars to be used in shipping the sheep required in the religious diet of the
Moslems of a French outfit coming through. Russell inquired if they were
part of the camel unit, and his commander wondered aloud if "Doc" had
indeed started the camel rumor that had spread for miles up and down the
railroad. Charlie Russell then beat a hasty retreat!

Two photos, U.S. Army

Railroad Magazine

Anglo-American Advance along the Railways

Even during their retreat the German forces made good use of the Italian State Railways. Field Marshal Albert Kesselring had ample time to execute phased withdrawals in most instances, and his railway and labor battalions performed admirably their task of repairing the ever-increasing air raid damage. When fifty thousand Anglo-American troops established a beachhead behind the German lines at Anzio on January 22, 1944, they caught Kesselring completely by surprise but failed to exploit the initiative. This momentary indecisiveness on the part of their commandant, the American Major General John P. Lucas, gave the Germans, under Hans von Mackensen, a chance to roll up the "Anzio Express," an aggregation of every available piece of railway artillery. While the huge railway guns pinned down the invaders and rail-mounted antiaircraft fire scattered their air cover, the Germans moved in reinforcements that held the expeditionary force to their landing zone for four months. By September 24 Sherman tanks of the 11th Canadian Armoured Regiment traversed a bulldozered path under the dangling tracks (*above*) of a bridge demolished by retreating Germans at Fantino. Italian railway troops, one wearing an American helmet (*upper right*) are shown clearing a bombed railroad yard near Civitavecchia on July 20. Bombed-out coaches were a welcome relief from muddy foxholes for soldiers of a tank destroyer battalion (*right*) who washed their clothes while keeping a loaded Springfield rifle and Thompson submachine gun close at hand, dangling from a door handle.

Variations on River Crossings

The backgrounds of the men who made up the MRS battalions affected their methods of rehabilitating the Italian State Railways. The 727th was sponsored by the Southern Railway, a line of many river bridges in the southeastern United States. The 713th, named "The Santa Fe Battalion," was under the sponsorship of that big western road. Because of the scarcity of water in much of the region, western railroaders prefer earth fills to bridging dry canyons, since bridges have to be maintained and often slow trains on account of speed restrictions. The photos on this spread show the approaches of both battalions to similar problems in Italy. In the photos *opposite* are shown the early stages of reconstruction of the Marta River bridge north of Civitavecchia in territory of the 727th. After dragging away the original bridge, which had been bombed out by the AAF, the Army built a standard military bridge over the Marta. First Sergeant Otis B. Schooley of "A" Company of the 713th chose the Santa Fe method of replacing a ten-arch, 320-feet-long, 90-feet-high bridge over the Savone River, near Sparanise, north of Naples. Schooley was awarded the Legion of Merit for his work on the fill (*above*), which is shown with the first through train (a load of desperately needed coal) between Naples and Rome. MRS officers, one with the familiar operating timetables in his pocket, stood in the foreground. Schooley performed an almost impossible task in coordinating the military and civilian efforts necessary to move over 120,000 yards of dirt for the fill, completing it in time to lend valuable logistical support to Fifth Army. These photos were taken on July 20, 1944, while just a few hundred miles away, *Wehrmacht* Colonel Klaus von Stauffenberg placed the bomb that narrowly missed killing Hitler in the now famous "Generals' Plot" to end the war. As in Sicily, the MRS troops in Italy captured large amounts of German Roth Wagner bridge sections. Using this standard bridging itself, or in conjunction with the equally renowned Bailey Bridging of the U.S. Army, the railroad troops were usually well stocked with bridge materials. The failure of the retreating Germans to destroy the stockpiles of bridging hastened their demise in the Italian campaign by enabling the railways to keep up with the Allied front.

Logistical Support for the Eighth Army

As the British Eighth Army advanced up the Adriatic coast of Italy, their own railway troops and engineer battalions restored the mutilated rail lines to service. The thoroughness with which the Germans incapacitated the railways was not enough to appreciably slow the Allied advance, and methods were devised to clear up the damage incredibly fast. The Germans would frequently blow the center out of every rail. Allied track crews merely cut off the damaged sections, slid the rails together, and after a few such sections, placed an additional length of rail in the gap. There were instances when German Army discipline was too successful, resulting in orders being followed to the letter with incredible proficiency, but unintended results. Such a case occurred at Aversa, where *Eisenbahnpionere* demolition teams carried out their orders to destroy the yard. They blew the center out of every second rail, placed demolition charges in car journals, and set the whole mess afire. That was the yard. Beyond the station, however, were ten carloads of brand new rails and ties that were untouched by the demolition teams! The yard was soon back in operation for the Allies. The British military railwaymen matched their Yank counterparts in rapid restoration work. Corporal D. H. Thorn, an ex-LNER man (*right*) gave hand signals to a crew shunting an unidentified Italian yard. A section gang supporting the Eighth Army (*below*) eased a new rail into position on January 4, 1944. As the Allies descended on Rome in June, 1944, sapper Raymond Akers (*lower right*) drilled tap holes for fastening sleepers (ties) in the final stages of replacing a masonry bridge in central Italy.

Three photos, Imperial War Museum

U.S. Army from Railroad Magazine

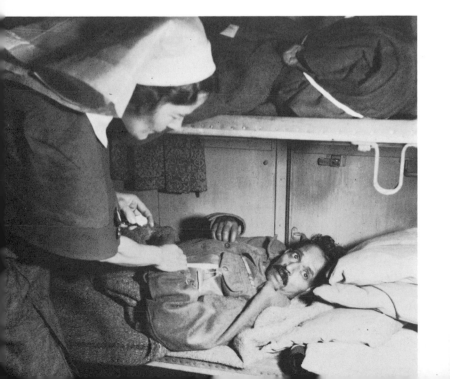

Restoring Men and Rails

Hospital trains were priority moves in every campaign, on both sides of the European war. On the Allied side, especially in a relatively static front such as Italy, these extra moves were carried out frequently and efficiently. The hospital cars, usually converted coaches (some were shipped over new from the United States) were distinguished by huge red crosses in white circles displayed on the roofs and car sides. Usually this practice was enough to deter hostile aircraft, although there were shameful exceptions. In 1944 GI Consolidation No. 1740 (*left*) was coupled to a train of newly converted Italian and German cars, while wounded troops, rushed down from the front, were transferred from ambulances at Riardo. The train was soon en route to the elaborate facilities of rear area hospitals and, for soldiers with "million dollar wounds," return to the States. Although their homeland was invaded by the Japanese in 1944, Indian troops were deployed with their British Empire comrades on virtually every front, including that of the Eighth Army in Italy. At Rome in February, 1945, two British nurses, Sisters Scobie and Aryes (*lower left*) served on board an Indian Army hospital train. Sister Aryes is shown (*far left*) tending a wounded Indian trooper. The war had already ended when the 136th Indian Railway Maintenance Company arrived in Bologna. The railway yards and shops had been a prime target of the Allied bombing offensive during Operation Strangle and were virtually annihilated. Within a month the efficient Indians had trains running through, and shortly thereafter, the station (*below*) was nearly rebuilt. A track gang of the 136th (*above left*) formed up for duty at the station, armed with rail tongs and spike mallets. Other men and officers of the company (*above*) posed on a wrecked Italian State Railways switch engine.

Operation Strangle

As the Allied armies slowly inched their way up the Italian peninsula during the winter of 1943–1944, German resistance stiff-
ened. It was estimated that the *Wehrmacht* needed three thousand
tons of supplies daily to conduct its operations. Since Mussolini had
built the Italian State Railways into one of the world's finest
systems, the mission of the German railway forces was relatively
uncomplicated, until the Allied commanders pinpointed the problem. On February 28, 1944, the Mediterranean Allied air forces
launched a furious aerial assault that was to pound the ISR
almost daily until the end of the war fourteen months later. The
mission of the American, British, and Free French airmen was to
strangle the supply lines to the German front through a phased
campaign. Primary concentration was to cut all the rail lines and
to continually harass restoration, forcing the German Army to
rely on road and coastal shipping. Since Germany's fuel reserves
were dangerously low and the Allies controlled the shipping lanes,
it was reasoned that German forces would quickly feel the pinch.
They did. First the marshalling yards in central Italy were hit,
forcing yard activities northward, then all of the major ports
and the scores of high railway bridges in northern Italy were cut.
Finally even the bridges in the Brenner Pass and other Alpine
crossings were wiped out, forcing the Germans into costly and
time-consuming transfers of cargo several times between rail and
highway transport. A flight of 12th Air Force Martin B-26 Marauders (*above*) dropped their loads of four 1,000-pound bombs
per plane on a railway bridge in the Po River valley. On November
22, 1944, a P-47 Thunderbolt dropped a demolition bomb on an
Italian rail line, scoring a direct hit (*right*), but the force of the
explosion caught the hapless craft, hurtling it a thousand feet
into the air and whipping it out of control. A few moments later
a following P-47 pilot snapped this melancholy scene of the bomb
crater and the burning Thunderbolt farther down the line. One of
the toughest jobs assigned to the fighter-bombers was the destruction of the vital Cecina River bridge. The wing of a P-47 lying
in a bomb crater at Cecina (*left*) testified to the damage suffered
by both sides.

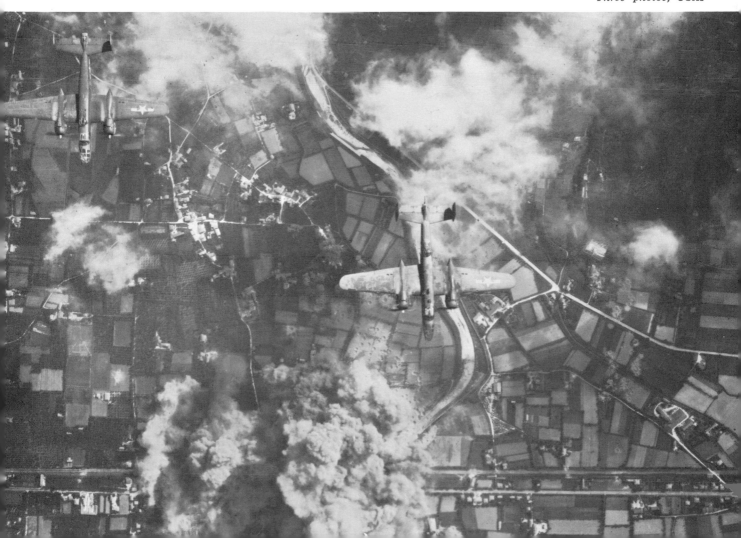

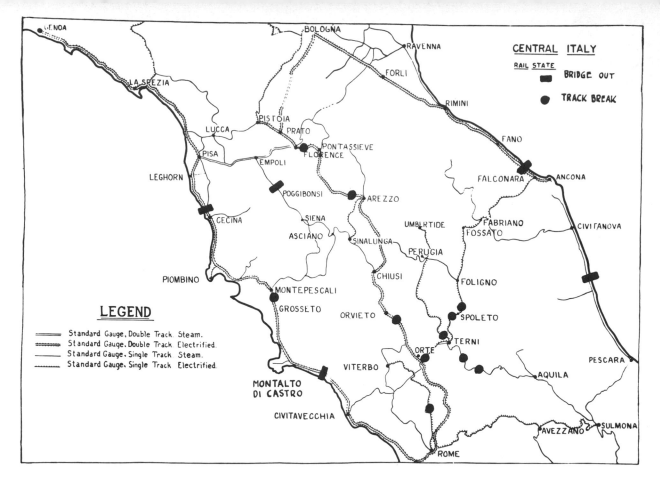

Map legend:

CENTRAL ITALY

RAIL STATE
- ▬ BRIDGE OUT
- ● TRACK BREAK

LEGEND

- ═══ Standard Gauge, Double Track, Steam.
- ═══ Standard Gauge, Double Track, Electrified.
- ─── Standard Gauge, Single Track, Steam.
- ∙∙∙∙ Standard Gauge, Single Track, Electrified.

Bridge-Busting B-25's

Perhaps the most famous medium bomber of World War II was the North American B-25 Mitchell, which saw extensive service in the Mediterranean and South Pacific theaters. They flew thousands of sorties during Operation Strangle and by early 1945 were paying regular visits to the bridges in the Brenner Pass (*upper left and below*), where rail communications were severed. At Pietrasanta, twenty miles north of Pisa, B-25's of the 1st Tactical Air Force (*left*) destroyed both a rail bridge and a paralleling highway structure. Most of the bridges in northern Italy were magnificent stone and masonry arch structures, as durable as they were beautiful. Repeated attacks, however, brought them all down. By March 24, 1944, a month after the start of Operation Strangle, an AAF map (*above*) showed the results of the early operations of the sustained aerial offensive.

Locomotive Casualties

While bridges, tunnels, engine terminals, and marshalling yards were the primary railway targets of any concerted aerial offensive against transportation networks, moving trains were quite lucrative and, to cocky young fighter-bomber pilots, a sort of sporting departure from the routine of hitting stationary targets. Train-busting often turned into a game of cat-and-mouse as P-47's hopped over the mountains and into the valleys searching for trains while railway engineers would dodge from tunnel to tunnel to avoid the bombs. Frequently, if Allied aircraft chased a train into a tunnel, the pilots would fly around to the opposite portal, come roaring up the track at fifty feet altitude and drop their bombs right in front of the portal. In the manner of the "skip-bombing" techniques of the Navy, the missles would bounce along the tracks, into the tunnel and hit the front of the locomotive. If the train was in a long tunnel, the frustrated pilots would drop their bombs right above both portals, causing landslides that sealed the entire train inside for hours, effectively blocking the line. The remnants of an Italian locomotive (*above left*) showed the results of Allied precision bombing. A hundred-pound general-purpose bomb went right through the top of the boiler (hole behind steam dome) of an engine in the yards in Florence. It exploded among the tubes, tearing the entire center out of the boiler. Here an AAF officer and an Italian railway man measure the five-foot gap in the boiler. Unusually clear for a gun-camera photo, the back-lighted picture (*above*) shows a German locomotive at the instant its boiler exploded in a splendor of spewing steam. At this moment the engine was being racked with direct twenty-millimeter cannon shellfire. Some B-25's were equipped with a seventy-five millimeter cannon in the nose and sent out engine-hunting. A hit from a seventy-five usually created a violent explosion, causing the boiler to go off with the force of a five-hundred-pound bomb. Unfortunately thousands of civilian enginemen on all sides were killed in these encounters. Later in the war, when the *Luftwaffe* had been conquered, P-38's and P-51's joined in the train-busting tactics, but most of these missions were flown by Republic P-47's. One such Thunderbolt pilot was Lieutenant Edward Syszmanski, the "Mad Pollack of Brooklyn." In one typical three-day period, he blew up thirteen and damaged four steam locomotives. Syszmanski described his technique to the press: "I come in from the back of the train, aiming at the third car from the engine. I watch the bullets creep up toward the locomotive, and my plane is usually about twenty-five feet above the cars before I get enough shots into the boiler. Some of the locos blow up a few feet and settle back on the tracks as if having a big sigh. Others just puke steam—I only claim them as damaged." Such tactics seriously hampered the Axis war effort and soon caused a massive reduction in daylight train movements.

Who's Surrendering to Whom?

On May 2, 1945, the German armies in northern Italy, pushed back to the Alps by the Allied offensives and cut off from their sources of supply by Operation Strangle, surrendered unconditionally. Only five years earlier, Hitler and Mussolini traveled by rail on several occasions to meet at the Brenner Pass, at the peak of their careers. By May 4, 1945, when hundreds of thousands of Germans were laying down their arms, American soldiers of the Fifth and Seventh Armies met at the Brenner Pass railway station (*above*), which had been rendered inoperative months before by Allied air raids. The Axis powers had been defeated in the field and from within; Hitler and Mussolini had both met violent deaths barely a week earlier; and a war-weary world reeled from the rapidity of the cataclysmic events since 1940. At San Michele, Italy, two German Army engineer officers (*below*), who had been rebuilding a railway bridge destroyed by 15th Air Force bombers, chatted amicably with AAF Lieutenant Colonel Jack D. Nichols at the time of the surrender. Nichols was armed only with a camera; the *Wehrmacht* officers were still wearing loaded automatic pistols. It is difficult to distinguish victor from vanquished in this photograph.

From Normandy to the Rhine

By the time of the D-Day invasion of Normandy by Allied armies on June 6, 1944, the *Société Nationale des Chemin de fer Français* —the French National Railways (SNCF)—had been so heavily damaged by Allied air attacks and the sabotage of the French Underground that German strategy could no longer depend on rail service for logistics. This factor was of vital consideration as both sides prepared for the campaigns that resulted in the complete destruction of the Third Reich. The German policy of stripping the SNCF of much of its motive power and rolling stock was another factor in the chaotic supply situation facing *Wehrmacht* field commanders. With the overwhelming Allied air forces regarding the SNCF as the principal target in France ever since 1942, virtually every locomotive belatedly sent from Germany after D-Day became a hunted prize.

As the Allied forces broke out of their tenuous beachheads and spread across France, their railway battalions, relatively secure under skies generally ruled by friendly air power, worked furiously and successfully to keep up with the advancing armies, even to the extent of operating trains before the roads were cleared in some sectors.

"Bomb Flower"

Two weeks after American forces broke out of the Saint-Lô pocket on July 26, 1944, U.S. railroad engineers surveyed the heavily damaged yard at Canisy. The locomotive had received a direct hit from a five-hundred-pound allied bomb during the huge aerial offensive that all but reduced the French railways to impotency. With boiler plates resembling the opening petals of a flower and the disheveled tubing reminiscent of a blossom's filaments, this locomotive was symbolic of the condition of the entire SNCF at the time— thoroughly devasted, but out of the ruination, hope for a promising future.

Black Star

American War Engines Destined for France

Once the Battle of Britain thwarted a German invasion and the United States entered the conflict, it became evident to both sides that England would be turned into a huge fortified military supply dump from which the assault on *Festung Europa* would be launched. Beginning in 1942, an overwhelming armada of ships, aircraft, men, weapons, trucks, and railway equipment was assembled in the British Isles. The first contingent of standard U.S. Army 2-8-0 Consolidation locomotives to arrive from the States (*upper left*) was unloaded at Morpeth Dock, Birkenhead, in November, 1942. The following month, No. 1604 (*above*) became the first of the 130-ton engines to be fired up and was operated with appropriate Anglo-American ceremonies at Paddington Station, as it was dispatched to haul its first British train. With a combined engine and tender length of sixty-one feet, these locomotives did some work on British rail lines while awaiting shipment to France. No. 1606 (*below*) was assigned to a hospital train, while others hauled freight and passengers, relieving native British engines for shipment to other zones of operation, such as Iran. An interesting comparison of the famous 1604 (*left*) with a standard British War Department 0-6-0 (*lower left*) shows the radically different interpretations given to the design of a general-purpose, standardized austerity locomotive by American and English builders.

Four photos, British Railways

British Railways

Three photos, U.S. Army

Tank Engines and Mass Production

The standard American switching locomotive, built in lesser numbers than the 2-8-0's, was an 0-6-0T design. One of them was photographed being unloaded at Cardiff docks (*upper left*) in December, 1943, while a sister, assigned to the British War Department (*above*) was reinforced by a truck that had been converted to railway use to switch the interiors of warehouses, reducing the fire hazard. Another "W-D" 0-6-0T was operated by men of the U.S. 761st Transportation Co. and other American railwaymen (*left*) mass-produced box-cars from prefabricated sections made in the U.S.A.

151

The Battle of Production

One of the greatest mistakes of the Axis leaders was their underestimation of the productive power of the United States. While supplying much of the Allies' weapons and material, American industry managed to turn out thousands of locomotives for both foreign and domestic service. Other nations, especially Germany, enjoyed this capability, but only the United States could do it on such a sustained basis and free from war damage. There are certain basic requirements for military locomotives. They must be adaptable (U.S. forces operated railways in temperatures ranging from 67 degrees below zero in Alaska to 147 degrees above in Iran). They must be as uncomplicated and maintenence-free as possible. They must rely heavily on standardized, interchangeable parts or on crude substitutes fabricated right in the field. They must be extremely durable and be able to absorb great punishment, including deferred or no maintenance and inferior grades of fuel. The last point raises a paradox, for military engines are not generally suited for civilian operations, so their useful life is extremely short: perhaps as little as one or two years—but brutal years! In spite of this short lifespan (steam locomotives were in service for up to fifty years), they had to be of the finest quality. The standard American "GI" 2-8-0, manufactured in the thousands by the three major U.S. builders—Baldwin, American, Lima— was an ideal military engine, and by D-Day over eight hundred of them were stored in England, ready for shipment to the Continent. Just a few weeks earlier, 2-8-0's under the care of the 756th Railway Shop Battalion at Ebbw Junction Depot in Newport, Wales (*below*), were fired up, repaired, and greased for the final check before crossing the Channel. At Penrhos Junction, Caerphilly, Wales (*left and lower left*), hundreds of the U.S. "war babies" were stored.

Three photos, U.S. Army

Allied Air Power Ravages the SNCF

Although the French railways had been an important target for the United States Army Air Force ever since a dozen Flying Fortresses flew the first 8th Air Force raid against *Festung Europa* by

bombing the Sotteville railway yards on August 17, 1942, it was early in April, 1944, that the methodical destruction of the SNCF began in earnest. For two months the medium and heavy bombers and the fighter-bombers of the 8th and 9th Air Forces flew thousands of sorties against the SNCF and Belgian rail facilities daily, when weather permitted. By D-Day three quarters of the two thousand locomotives in northern France had been put out of service by this airpower. Of the twenty-four railway bridges spanning the Seine from Paris northwest, eighteen were destroyed and three heavily damaged, including one (*left*) the destruction of which not only prevented supplies from reaching German combat units, but hampered their orderly retreat as well. Prior to the invasion (code-named Operation Overlord) 9th Air Force medium bombers waged a furious battle with the *Luftwaffe* and antiaircraft, including the flak towers that the Germans had erected in France, to defend such vital targets as the SNCF. The Douglas A-20 Havocs, with wings and fuselages black-and-white striped for the invasion, bombing Damfront, France (*right*), and the Martin B-26 Marauders (*above*), 150 of which plastered the huge triangular-shaped marshalling yard at Namur, Belgium, on April 10, bore the brunt of the attacks on German communications leading to the Normandy beaches.

The Tally of Destruction

The roster of motive power of the French National Railways in early 1940 showed about 17,000 active locomotives. As the *Wehrmacht* was pushed back toward the Rhine, fewer than 3,000 remained operable. Five thousand locomotives had been commandeered by the Germans for service in occupied territory throughout the Reich. Of the remaining total, over 2,700 were destroyed by the French Resistance and 6,000 by Allied air attacks. Over half of the more than 500,000 SNCF freight cars and 20,000 passenger cars had been taken by the Germans. Thousands more were destroyed from the air. In electrified territory over 1,000 miles of catenary was destroyed, along with one-third of the 66 power substations. Tens of thousands of SNCF workers were sent to work the German rail facilities, especially in prime target areas. Twenty thousand never returned from captivity.

Three photos, USAF

Rails across the Beachhead

The horrendous destruction of the French railways was well known to Eisenhower's headquarters, and elaborate plans had been laid to put three U.S. Army Railway Grand Divisions and five Operating and three Shop Battalions ashore soon after D-Day to effect emergency repairs to the mainlines on the axis of the Allied advances. British railway units also began to take over sections of track in their sectors. Within thirty-five days of the invasion, when the Allies had moved just twenty-five miles inland, railway rolling stock and locomotives began arriving at the beaches from England. LST (landing ship tanks) invasion craft such as No. 21 were laid with railroad track and loaded with up to twenty-two pieces of rolling stock at a time (*left*) in British ports. At Normandy the railway cars were sent ashore via floating bridgework (*above and upper right*), which was designed to compensate for the twenty-eight-foot tides of the Channel. Tracks had been laid right across the sand and connected to the SNCF, and the beaches were the only source of railway and all other vital supplies during the perilous early weeks of invasion, before the capture and return to service of the ports of Cherbourg and LeHavre. By mid-October over 20,000 cars, most of them loaded with military cargo, and 1,300 locomotives had crossed the Channel from England; 11,288 cars and 702 locomotives arrived via the LST and LCT car ferries—the floating link between British and French rails. Small British diesel engines (*right*) were unloaded by tractors on the British Second Army beachhead on July 26.

Three photos, U.S. Coast Guard

Imperial War Museum

The Trickle Becomes a Flood

Within five weeks after the capture of Cherbourg, the port and rail facilities had been repaired enough to permit the unloading of American locomotives directly from oceangoing vessels. On August 1, 1944, GI 2-8-0 No. 2867 (*below*) was swung ashore while 0-6-0T No. 6009, unloaded previously, stood by. While the U.S. engines were coming ashore, an ancient French puffer (*left*) with a vertical boiler occupied an adjoining track. The engines that had been stored in England were prepared weeks before the invasion for immediate action: each one arrived in France with water in the boiler, paper and tinder in the firebox, and coal and water in the tender. Some of the U.S. boxcars (*upper right*) that operated at the front sported gaudy camouflage. As casualties mounted, both German and Allied wounded were brought to Cherbourg by rail, where they were transferred to ambulances (*lower right*) for the journey to the waterfront and ultimately, to hospitals in England. The two maps dramatically illustrate the affect of the war on the SNCF; over 80 per cent of the prewar rail lines were destroyed by D-Day. What remained existed in small disconnected sections, with Paris, Lyons, Marseilles, Lille, and other major cities totally inacessible by rail.

Two photos, U.S. Army

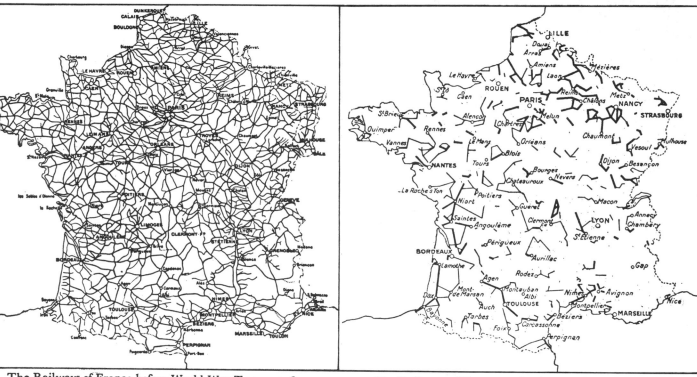

The Railways of France before World War Two – 1936

Maps from Railways in Wartime, *by E. F. Carter, Fred. Muller, Ltd.*

The Railways of France at the time of Liberation, 1944

Two photos, Railroad Magazine

Three photos, U.S. Army

Endless Wreckage

On June 23, 1944, just seventeen days after the initial assault, the yard at Croiden was already functioning for the Allies when the *Luftwaffe* paid a two A.M. visit. By the end of the day French workers (*above*) had almost completed the task of track repair. On September 12 the yards in Laon (*upper right*) presented a scene of heavy damage that had been inflicted by Allied bombers during the spring "softening up" of the French railways. On May 7 and in subsequent raids, U.S. bombers dealt the huge enclosed roundhouse at Mohon (*right*) severe blows. Although most of the rubble had been cleared when the Allies arrived in September, no rebuilding had been attempted. Like many organizations in the war, the American Military Railway Service had its own publication, entitled *The Yankee Boomer*. Appropriately, the masthead (*below*) portrayed an American soldier with lantern and .45 calibre automatic. Many times railway troopers of all belligerents had to turn from railroading to take up arms against the enemy.

The Long Road Back to the Rhine

Once the German Army was in full retreat, as it was on all fronts by July, 1944, photographs of its operations became scarce and photos of railway movements virtually nonexistent, especially in France, where railway activity had been so greatly curtailed. At least one *Panzer* unit, however, managed to utilize a rail line (*left*) during its retreat across France in the summer of 1944. By May 22, 1944, two weeks before the initial landings and over three months before the liberation of Paris, the railway situation in the capital (*above*) was one of utter desolation, as Allied airpower obliterated every facility that was of use to the *Wehrmacht*. On August 15 Allied forces invaded the Mediterranean coast of France near Marseilles and drove up the Rhone Valley to Lyons and a linkup with Allied armies, which were liberating the north. With much of the Italian rail system back in civilian control, several American railway battalions were pulled out of "the boot," and within a month after the capture of the port of Marseilles on August 28, bridges had been rebuilt, rubble cleared, and track and rolling stock repaired to the extent that regular service was opened to Lyons. Beginning just five weeks after that, the MRS dispatched 415,404 net tons over this line, utilizing 32,951 carloads in 716 train movements, during the month of November, 1944. As in Italy, the Germans used a "big hook scarifier" to tear up track in France. The work of the track ripper and the hook itself is shown after its capture (*below*) by American forces on the line from Falquemont to Avold, in Alsace-Lorraine, during the winter of 1944-45.

Two photos, Donald P. Kane

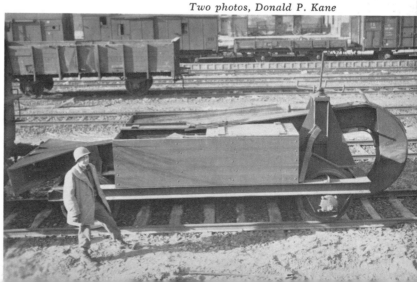

Charles D. Russell

J. L. McBride

Clearing All Manner of Problems

Railway facilities and equipment, with their many far-flung installations, are favorable to defenders, especially snipers, as the apprehensive Canadians (*left*) found when they overcame the last German resistance in the Vaucelles rail yard on August 7, 1944. The Germans abandoned a lightly armored flak train (*lower left*) at Sarrebourg, Lorraine, so quickly that they even left the guns intact. Allied train wrecks were not always caused by hostile action. A rear-end collision at Lourches (*above*) at Christmastime led a sarcastic GI railroader to letter No. 2845's tender accordingly. An American hospital train (*right*) was derailed on December 8, 1944, when it hit a huge steel wire mat, which apparently had fallen off a passing freight. On November 28 German prisoners (*below*) were loaded into French "forty and eight" boxcars at Epinal for shipment to the rear.

Donald P. Kane

U.S. Army

Stopping Von Rundstedt's Counteroffensive

Once the Germans ascertained the extent of the Allied assault, Von Rundstedt launched a counteroffensive in a vain attempt to push the invaders back to the Channel. Ninth Air Force fighters and bombers went on a rampage, interdicting every supply line, including routes of the SNCF that the Germans had recently returned to service through Herculean efforts. Within a few days, the German front was virtually isolated from its source of supply and Patton's armor was breaking through. One of the *Reichsbahn* locomotives brought from Germany to augment the depleted engine roster of the SNCF was caught on a bridge over the Moselle River (*right*) and when reached by Allied infantry was still balanced precariously on the collapsed span. Hundreds of tons of supplies in the train it was pulling were also captured, never having reached Von Rundstedt's beleaguered forces. The engine terminal at Longveau (*below*) could offer little help to the Germans after a raid by the AAF. Carrying vitally needed Junker aircraft engines for the *Luftwaffe*, a train was captured by American troops at Charmes (*lower right*) on September 18, 1944, after a spirited firefight that left the tender of the French 4-6-0 riddled with bullet holes.

SNCF

French Railway Casualties

All through the occupation of France the SNCF personnel had worked closely with the Resistance to keep the Allies informed of German train movements. The courageous railwaymen who started vital information on its way to England were very aware that the resulting air raids might take their own lives. Whenever possible, the RAF and the AAF would warn the French of imminent air attacks by dropping flares at night or making one "dry-run" pass by day, before attacking, giving the train crew a chance to jump clear. Still, there were many casualties from the air raids. There were instances such as occurred on July 17, 1944, when Resistance fighters sabotaged track, holding up a trainload of German gasoline. They quickly radioed the Allies and within a few minutes AAF bombers had destroyed the train. Other acts of sabotage at the throats of marshalling yards trapped German trains long enough to call in Allied air strikes, or if the trains did reach the front, they were late by as much as two weeks. By March, 1944, the sabotage of the SNCF men had become so effective that the RAF began parachuting explosives, weapons, and ammunition to the railway Resistance fighters at night. That the French retained some measure of independence from the Germans is illustrated by the fact that when the Germans asked the French railway shop supervisors to repair French engines that had been expropriated to Germany, the French simply refused to accept the locomotives. When some engines were finally returned for such repairs, they were captured by the Allies!

USAF

U.S. Army

A Legacy of Destruction

As the Germans retreated, they attempted to destroy whatever motive power and rolling stock they had to leave behind. American railway soldiers (*below*), operating so close behind the front that they were still armed, surveyed the damage to the steam chest of a French engine blown apart by a demolition charge. Destruction of rail facilities in the south of France was the job of the 12th and 15th U.S. Army Air Forces, based in North Africa and Italy. Both Air Forces thoroughly worked over the Toulon yards (*left*) for the Allied invasion. When two carloads of beams were needed to repair a bridge north of Toulouse that had fallen victim to the Mediterranean U.S. Air Forces, the German Army conductor in charge of the movement was puzzled when the French brakeman had the electric locomotive on the train replaced with a steamer. "You don't know the French system," said the brakeman, "or you would realize that Langon, the initial destination of this run, is not electrified." Actually the train should have gone to Lanton, but the confused German agreed to send the train in the opposite direction, resulting in several days delay in reopening the bridge and ten days in the stockade for the hapless conductor, a typical victim of French cunning. Pierre Laval, the Vichy French leader, who was despised as a traitor by his countrymen, agreed to a weird plan for the repatriation, in 1942, of French soldiers who had been in Nazi POW camps since the 1940 capitulation. One POW was to be returned for every three healthy young French workers "recruited" to be sent to work in factories in Germany. The hundreds of thousands of Frenchmen involved in this exchange traveled by railway, the workers having twenty-four hours' notice of their departure for the Reich. The final statistics of liberation show that of 144 seriously damaged engine terminals, 77 were never returned to service by the Germans; 25 out of 40 marshalling yards were abandoned, as were 19 out of 33 major shop facilities and 120 out of 330 passenger stations.

U.S. Army

Beginning an Impossible Task

Engine terminals and shop facilities had been particularly lucrative targets to both the Allied air forces and the demolition teams of the retiring Germans. Although the retreating *Wehrmacht* had little time to demolish the locomotives at the Laval enginehouse (*above*), the AAF had left plenty of work for the American 764th and 755th Railway Shop Battalions, stationed east at Le Mans and west at Rennes, respectively, on the main line from Paris to Brest. It was appropriate that the locomotive with the shrapnel-ventilated stack fired up by men of "C" Company, 720th Railway Operating Battalion (*below*), was an American engine,

sent to France during World War I. On August 26 men of the 755th RSB, working with French shopmen as was the normal procedure, rode the first locomotive (*upper right*) to be repaired in the Rennes shop since liberation. A "V" for victory was chalked on the engine and some of the Americans still carried carbines as protection against isolated Germans who might have been bypassed by Patton's rapid push through the area two weeks before. The first MRS unit in France was the 729th ROB, which arrived in Cherbourg to take charge of the roundhouse (*lower right*) even before electric power was restored to the city, necessitating a bulldozer to operate the turntable.

Two photos, U.S. Army

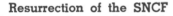

Resurrection of the SNCF

In spite of the vast devastation dealt the French railways, they were put back into operating shape so rapidly that both the German and the Allied high commands were amazed. In one instance a bridge was replaced an entire week ahead of the demanding schedule set for the job. Usually the French railwaymen were very cooperative, but a few, having finally been freed from German authority, were in no mood to take orders from any other foreigners, including their American liberators. The MRS standard solution for that problem was to draw a .45 or unshoulder a carbine and to cock it with a loud "clank." This method overcame all language barriers and differences of opinion. A favorite form of crippling a locomotive used by the Germans was to blow the cylinders apart with TNT. In Barisey La Côte many a member of the 733rd ROB was shocked to discover a French engine, its cylinders blown off and leaking steam in great quantities, nonchalantly puttering about its switching duties in the yard. This mechanical impossibility was reconciled by the fact that the engine was a four-cylinder compound and the two inboard cylinders functioned quite well, although half the steam generated by the boiler was escaping by way of what the Germans must have thought was a complete demolition job! Frenchmen began to clean up Nevers (*above*) while the first train to leave the heavily damaged yards in Laon

(*upper right*) was double-headed with a GI 2-8-0 leading an SNCF engine. Although sponsored by the Chicago & Northwestern, the 720th ROB had at least one loyal Pennsylvania Railroad man at Lison (*right*) who lettered a French engine after that line's crack *Broadway Limited.** A German light railway used to supply a *Luftwaffe* base, similar to that on page 37, was put to work by 9th Air Force crews (*below*) and the new tenants of the base, P-51 Mustangs of a fighter squadron.

* *The same class of locomotive appears on pages 146–147 and 169.*

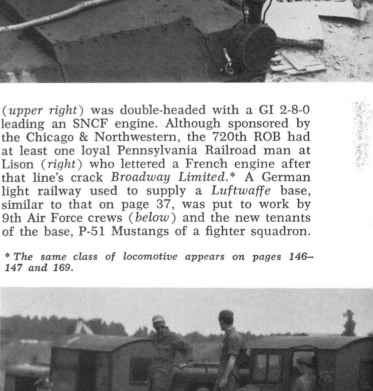

Trains versus Trucks in France

By the winter of 1944–45, France had become a vast staging area for the final assault on Germany itself. Railway lines, highways, canals, and airfields were all operating at peak capacity. The final lesson of logistics had been learned during the dash of Patton's Third Army across France. His advance had been so rapid, and the destruction of the SNCF so complete, that the famed *Red Ball Express* was organized to supply his forces by highway. At the peak of its operation this highway effort was bringing Patton 8,500 tons daily—the capacity of only fifteen French freight trains of that time and barely the capacity of an average train operating in the United States! This effort so taxed the vehicles and men that both soon began

to wear out, resulting in serious accidents and ruin of the trucks from lack of maintenance. Also, driving the long distances (up to four hundred miles), the trucks consumed much of their most precious cargo: gasoline. The official military history stated bluntly: *"Red Ball* was carried out at a terrible cost." In a short time twice the amount of freight carried by *Red Ball* was handled by the SNCF with little strain on men, equipment, or railroad, and within a few months the tonnage had increased twelvefold! If Patton developed an affection for the MRS in Sicily, he was all the more delighted when abundant supplies of gasoline for his tanks began arriving by rail (*above*) via SNCF as he drove toward the Rhine. Doubleheaded MRS diesels (*below*) brought a hospital train past a

Three photos, U.S. Army

freight. In 1945 the MRS began operation of the *Toot Sweet Special* to carry top-priority freight at express schedules to the front. The commander of the 728th ROB, Lieutenant Colonel Carl D. Love, issued orders to the crew of the *Special* prior to its departure from Cherbourg (*upper right*) on February 10, 1945. One of the engine crews of the Military Railway Service solution to highway logistics problems (*right*) is shown waiting for the "highball" to roll the *Toot Sweet* (an Americanization of the French *"tout de suite"*—"right quick")

toward the front. The cartoon is the work of Glen E. Blomberg, artist laureate of the 713th and an operating man who had worked for the Chicago, Burlington & Quincy Railroad in Denver.

Railroad Magazine

OUR INTRODUCTION TO A FRENCH ENGINE

Yankee Boomers in France

In American railroad slang a "boomer" is a man who has worked on many railroads. To the 22,000 men of the twenty-eight U.S. Army Railway Operating and Shop Battalions, as well as thousands more in Engineer Headquarters, and other units that had served in France by 1945, a boomer was judged by the number of countries in which he railroaded—United States, Morrocco, Algeria, Tunisia, Sicily, Italy, England, France, and for most of them, on to Germany. A few eventually wound up in the Philippines, Korea, China, and Japan, plus other areas covered elsewhere in this volume. In eight and a half months preceding the surrender of Germany alone, the Americans moved more than eighteen million tons of military freight, plus hundreds of thousands of troops, POW's, and the needs of the civilian population over the SNCF. Part of the credit for this vast accomplishment is due to the rapport between American and French military forces (*left*) and U.S. Army and French railroaders (*above*), who worked together for a common cause. Americans from many units, such as the fireman of an oil-burning 733rd ROB GI engine (*below*) and the American conductor blowing a Belgian railway horn in a German caboose with a French guard on SNCF rails (*right*) operated by the 740th ROB, contributed a major effort toward the final victory.

Four photos, U.S. Army

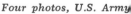

The Fall of the Third Reich

By the beginning of the year 1943 all the great victories of Nazi Germany were behind her. Ahead lay only defeat, destruction, and death for millions of hapless soldiers and civilians alike, who had absolutely no control over the fate that irresistibly pulled them into history's most ruthless trap. The Allies knew it, as did many Germans in the field who saw the results of the growing strength of their enemies first-hand. The German population, fed ever-increasing dosages of "German invincibility" propaganda and Allied bombs, were confused. Only Hitler and his lieutenants and their closest followers had succumbed to the "Big Lie" of their own creation. Propaganda Minister Joseph Goebbels had propagated the theory of the "Big Lie": if a lie is big enough and told often enough, people will begin to believe it. Goebbels himself had become the most interesting victim of his own theory!

If Germany's paths to victory were laid with steel rails, so were those of her conquerors. No

Night Fire on the Eastern Front

A machine gun on an armor-plated car of a Red Army train is shown spewing fire and hot steel as it cut a swarth through the Russian winter night in support of one of the many Soviet counter-offensives that pounded relentlessly at the German Army, pushing it steadily back toward the frontiers of its homeland.

Sovfoto

slackers themselves in the ability to produce railway equipment, the Germans were surpassed in 1943 by the rapidly increasing industrial might of their adversaries and the alarming tempo at which their railway plant and the means to replace it were being consumed by their own needs and by squadrons, wings, and finally overwhelming armadas of heavy bombers that began pounding the Third Reich. Through it all, however, railways of the *Deutsche Reichsbahn* and the military lines and railroads in occupied countries continued to function. In spite of the severe dislocations imposed by such concerted enemy efforts as Operation Strangle in Italy, beginning in 1944, there never occurred—except in northern France after D-Day—a total breakdown in rail transport. From that point of view the massive, costly Allied aerial offensives were as futile as had been the assault of the *Luftwaffe* on England. The inherent recuperative powers of railway transport worked well for Germany. Although the hampering of railway activity wrought by the Allied aerial bombardment may have been worth the cost, it was only after the victorious Allied armies, closing on Germany from east, west, and south, actually occupied the terrain and drove the *Wehrmacht* out, that the railways ceased being of use to Germany and immediately became the avenues of her destruction.

Annihilation at Stalingrad

The colossal struggle for the Volga River industrial center of Stalingrad (since renamed Volgograd by the Soviet government), which began when the deepest penetration of Russia by German forces arrived there the end of August, 1942, became the worst defeat in the history of Germany. A little over five months later, the entire German Sixth Army, one of the best in the world, consisting of nearly one third of a million men, had been surrounded, starved, and beaten into surrender. Half the men had been killed; most of the rest died in prison camps. Only those fortunate enough to have been severely wounded early in the fighting were air-evacuated and returned to their homeland.

Once surrounded, its railway communications to Germany securely in Russian hands, the mighty Sixth Army began to die, forbidden by Hitler to retreat while a breakthrough was still possible. Russian soldiers, attacking from a railroad embankment (*upper left*), helped tighten the noose around Stalingrad. All rail lines leading into the city were torn up by the Germans, who used the track materials to build tank obstacles. Red troops (*lower left*) swarm down the platforms toward the main depot building. After the German surrender of the city, captured *Panzer* tanks were loaded on flatcars (above), and the pitiful remnants of the Sixth Army (*below*) were put to work rebuilding the railways.

Photoworld

The "People's Avengers" Strike

Once the Russians came to regard the German invasion as that of oppressors, rather than the hoped-for liberators, they turned on the Germans with a furious vengeance. Organized into guerrilla units behind the German lines, they struck often and hard at the vulnerable lines of communication, concentrating on the omnipotent railways. A unit of "People's Avengers," as they were known, is shown fleeing a lonely German railway outpost (*upper left*) under fire, after a raid that nearly wiped out the facility. A favorite target was the *Panzerzugen*—armored trains—of the German Army, such as the one whose locomotive (*lower left*) was blown fifty feet by a tremendous explosion. Red Army railway troops on the 3rd Byelorussian Front in July, 1944, investigated the possibilities of clearing the wreckage. Cossacks from the Kuban area of the Caucasus looked over the smoldering wreckage of an armored train (*above*) that they had successfully destroyed. Barbed wire obstructions, blockhouses, patrols, all failed to halt the "Avengers" as they struck the German-held railways at times and places of their choosing. A typical method was to place explosives beneath the rail joints. A delayed-fuze device would cause several charges to blow at once, after the entire train (*below*) had entered the mined section.

Insecure Communications

Large forces of German security troops were engaged in a sometimes losing battle to keep supplies flowing to their armies on the Russian front. Motorized patrols, such as the one shown (*left*) jumping for cover behind a trackside shanty while under fire, continuously roamed the long rail lines of Russia. So many tracks and bridges were mined that locomotives frequently pushed cars loaded with sand ahead of them (*upper left*) to absorb the shock of explosions and enable engines to stop before reaching the blown track sections. While hundreds of Russians, such as paratroopers (*above*) planted explosives, thousands of Germans, like this railway soldier (*below*), sought out the charges, to remove them. An example of the disruption caused by these tactics occurred when a Russian ski trooper, hearing an approaching German patrol, fled into a nearby field before he could cover the mine he had just planted. Before the Germans could remove it, a train approached. The soldiers fired into the air to alert the engineer. Thinking he was being attacked, the engineer pulled the throttle harder as the train guards nervously opened fire. The resulting explosion wrecked the train and caused thirty casualties, witnessed by the Russian, who lay camouflaged in the snow fifty yards away.

Three photos, Sovfoto

Russian Roadbed Restoration

Once the Red Army had cleared the Germans from an area, there was usually much railway repair work to be done. One advantage the Soviets had in fighting on their own terrain was that railway operations could be turned over to the civilian crews immediately, relieving the military to concentrate on the task of repair work. The Red Army tables of organization in World War II called for several types of railway units. The most common were the Railway Restoration Battalions, comparable to U.S. Army Engineer units, except that they were concerned exclusively with railway work and handled projects on highways or other construction only in emergencies. Railroad Troops in organized units were responsible for guarding such railway installations as bridges, tunnels, stations, and strategic sections of track. It is probable that they also manned the weapons on board the armored trains. For purely military railways and for service in foreign countries that the Russians took from the Germans, railway operating units were also employed. It must also be recalled that all civilian railway workers in the Soviet Union during wartime are "militarized" and under the strict control of the Army. Soldiers of a Restoration Battalion (*above*) are shown repairing track on the edge of the Sea of Azov near the junction at Taganrog in September, 1943, while a camouflaged armored train stood guard, since this was still disputed territory. The Germans standard-gauged the broad Russian track by moving one rail three and a half inches inward to take their equipment along the main lines of advance. As the Communists recaptured it, they would simply return the rail to its original position. For areas of counteroffensives the track gauge might be changed a half dozen times. Occasionally the Germans would use power saws to cut the ends off the ties as they left, forcing the Russians to replace the ties before the track could be broad-gauged again. The photo of Soviet troops altering track gauge (*below*) was supposedly made under German fire. In view of the fact that the explosion has already been spent and the earth clods are falling back down, the "enemy shell" was probably staged for the photographer. Had a shell really landed so close, wartime instincts and experience would have caused the men to automatically "hit the dirt!"

Quick Repairs
When German bombers scored near misses on an armored train, its crew repaired tracks damaged in the attack in an hour. Flak guns on the train and the arrival of Soviet fighters drove off the *Luftwaffe* aircraft before they could make a second pass at the train.

Two photos, Bundesarchiv

Belgian Royal Army Museum

Final German Efforts in Russia

With the battered *Wehrmacht* in full but orderly retreat on the Russian front in 1944, it was vital to keep the railway lines open. Because of the danger of big Soviet offensives, the Germans took great care to keep the railways—their most vital avenue of escape to the west—in good condition. In the summer of their retreat into Central Europe, a regiment of *Eisenbahnpioniere* stood in formation (*lower right*) during the ceremonies commemorating the restoration of a vital railway bridge. The latest known German wartime military railway photograph, taken on August 16, 1944, shows military railwaymen using a Russian engine (*upper right*) to weight-test a temporary timber span. Armored trains, mounting medium-caliber guns (*above and left*) covered the withdrawals. The locomotive on the eastern front in 1944 (*below*) was an excellent example of a heavily armored German engine. There are dozens of access doors in the armor plating for maintenence of the machine.

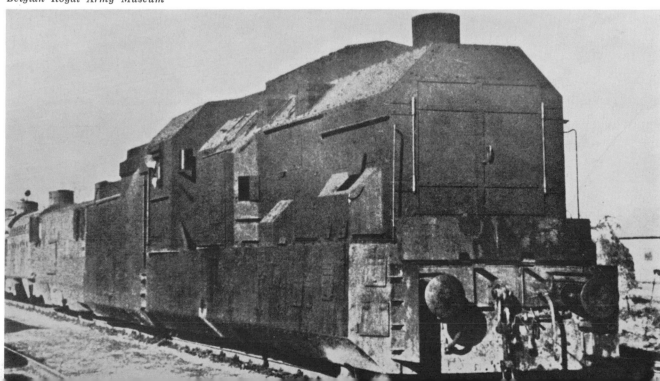

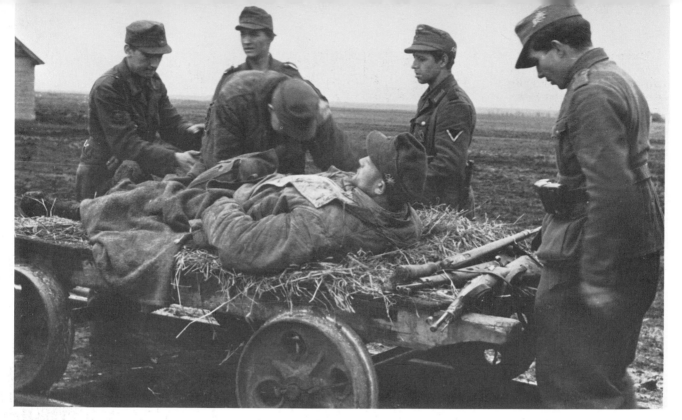

Evacuation by Rail

The three phases of evacuation by rail for wounded German troops were demonstrated (*at left, top to bottom*) on the eastern front. With a railroad track close to the combat area, one wounded soldier was placed on a straw-covered handcar trailer, while another was assisted aboard by two medics. The ruthlessness of the campaigns in the east dictated that even medical teams be armed, hence the *Mauser* carbines on the car. Another phase of medical evacuation was from ambulance to boxcar, but in rear areas roomy and well-lit hospital trains were often used. One of the notorious "trackwolf scarifiers" is shown in action (*right and below*) ripping up broadgauge Russian track. After demolishing the ties of one track of a double-track mainline (*lower right*), the scarifier, pulled by several locomotives, disappeared over the horizon. Soon it returned, ravaging the second track on its course of destruction, as other soldiers cut down the paralleling power and communication lines.

Five photos, Bundesarchiv

Reoccupying the Railways

As the Soviet Army recaptured ever-widening areas of its German-occupied western regions, Railway Restoration Battalions swarmed over the wrecked rail lines and with the assistance of Engineers, labor units, *Wehrmacht* prisoners, and penal companies, quickly had the trains operating again. The penal companies were made up of convicted military felons, who were considered the most expendable individuals in a military establishment that was notoriously careless of its human resources, resulting in a battlefield casualty ratio which favored the Germans better than four to one. A penal company was called up, for example, if a mine field posed an obstruction to the rapid repair of a vital railway. The hapless convicts cleared the mine field by the simple expedient of marching through it! Red Army trench mortar crews (*above*) moved their weapons through the devastated railway terminal in Kharkov during their counterattack on the city in February, 1943. Back in Lithuania by October, 1944, and driving toward Königsberg on the frontier of East Prussia, Soviet troops (*left*) attacked from under a train on the 1st Baltic Front. A German shell had just blown the boxcar behind them off the rails, setting it afire and flushing out other Russian soldiers who were under it. This photo was taken at the railway junction northwest of Siauliai, on the line to Telsiai and the Baltic coast. Guarding against aerial attacks by the *Luftwaffe* or the Finnish Air Force on the Karelian front, Soviet gunners manning the standard 12.7-millimeter heavy machine gun (*right*) were deployed in both armor-plated and wooden cars. Note the mouthpiece used for steadying the spotter's binoculars.

Three photos, Sovfoto

Wheels Roll Nowhere

Relentlessly the Soviet onslaught pushed the mortally wounded *Wehrmacht* westward to complete catastrophe. All along the desperately fought lines

of retreat, German engineers (*above*) placed demolition charges and strung detonator wire to blow their bridges behind them. By July, 1944, the Germans were evacuating Bialystok, one of their central-Poland jumping-off points for the invasion of Russia a few weeks more than three years earlier. Warsaw lay just one hundred miles to the rear. The facade of the Bialystok depot (*left*) had already been hit by Russian fire, but the *Deutsche Reichsbahn* motto of the war was still displayed under the station sign, above the main entrance: "Wheels Must Roll for Victory." These signs had been posted at rail facilities throughout the Reich, and the conquering Allies frequently found them among the twisted wreckage of Germany's railways. Out behind the station there was no thought of victory, or rolling wheels, as demolition teams (*below and right*) prepared the charges that brought a pedestrian overpass crashing down on the mainline tracks.

The Railways of Europe and the "Field Engines" of Germany during the Third Reich

In 1937 the *Deutsche Reichsbahn* was working at its peacetime capacity, with full employment and a high utilization of all equipment. Although operating on a war footing by 1939, the invasion of Poland created a threefold problem. There was the immediate situation of organizing thousands of special train movements during August and September, in direct support of so massive a military venture as the Polish campaign, plus the continuing increased military traffic once the Allies declared war. At the same time, the British Royal Navy imposed a severe and successful blockade that virtually curtailed ocean travel for Axis-bound ships and severely limited much coastal traffic. An example of the latter was the fact that the one million tons of Ruhr coal required monthly to fuel Italian industry had to be transferred from principal dependence on barge transport to railway lines over the Alps after the loss of the African campaign greatly increased the Allies' hold on the Mediterranean. Added to these monumental transport demands was the fact that very strong restrictions on gasoline usage for all but military purposes forced most of the former highway traffic— passenger and freight—onto the German railway system.

The acute shortage of all natural fuels except coal also burdened the railway operating program, but fortunately for both England and Germany, the vast preponderance of their motive

power at the time consisted of coal-fired steam locomotives. Had either the British or the German railways been extensively dieselized, as they were to become later, it is doubtful that they could have accomplished their missions as well as they did—if at all. British railway author E. F. Carter, in his book *Railways in Wartime,* sums up the dangerous situation that confronts the strategic role of Britain's railways today, and once again proves that the painfully learned lessons of history are quickly forgotten. His words, applicable to all European railways and, to an extent, to those of North America and Asia as well, appear on page 211:

> . . . our mass transition from steam to oil driven railway motive-power can, in the event of any future upheaval, place our country at the mercy of the nations from which we import our locomotives' lifeblood—oil. Today it can be truly said that Britain has all its transport "eggs" in one basket, whilst home-produced coal, which does not demand precious shipping-space in wartime, is allowed to stock-pile to the tune of tens of millions of tons. . . .

A little-known lesson of the Russian railways is further proof; before World War II less than 1 per cent of their locomotive fuel consisted of wood. With the loss of the coal fields of the Donets Basin, that figure was raised to 11 per cent. Of paramount importance in wartime is the adaptability of rail-

Pionier-Schule

Pionier-Schule

way motive power. Under certain emergency conditions a steam locomotive can burn almost anything, as the Russians proved, yet virtually all the steam engines have been slated for demolition. Thousands of them should have been stored by a dozen countries for purposes of their own national security.

Because of the rapidly expanding areas of operations of the German railways, the problems of increased haulage and vastly increasing motive power and rolling stock requirements were partially offset by equipment requisitioned in occupied lands. Just one example was provided by the government of the Netherlands at the postwar Nuremberg trials of Nazi war criminals: "Of 890 locomotives (steam), 490 were requisitioned; of 30,000 freight cars, 28,950 were requisitioned; of 1,750 passenger cars, 1,446 were requisitioned; of 300 electric trains, 215 were requisitioned; of 37 diesel-engine trains, 36 were requisitioned. . . ." In addition, the report continued, what the Germans left was generally in bad repair or war-damaged. They also took much in the way of fixed-plant equipment.

The operation of virtually all of continental Europe's railways by the end of 1942 was not too great a drain on German railway manpower, since the administration of the lines, while under strict Nazi control, was handled at all lower levels by native management and operating personnel. One major exception was Russia, which consumed so much of the resources of the German nation, including the railway output. Paradoxically, the retreat of the German Army from deep penetrations beyond the borders of Germany significantly reduced the *Reichsbahn* area of operations, which was a great help, but it also concentrated the target areas for Allied bombers, which was to prove disastrous.

To augment the existing motive power of the *Reichsbahn* and that taken from the railways of occupied countries, German industry embarked on a massive locomotive-building campaign in 1942. While the United States and Great Britain relied on the 2-8-0 wheel arrangement for standard power, Germany had long favored the 2-10-0, with its greater hauling ability. During the three years from 1942 to 1945, 7,592 *Feldlokomotieven*—field locomotives—were erected by seven major companies in Germany, Czechoslovakia, and Poland. They were all 2-10-0's of Class 42 (19.8 U.S. tons axle load) and Class 52 (16.5 U.S. tons axle load). Most of these were built for service in Eastern Europe and, once the track gauge was altered, in Russia. There were 840 of the heavier Class 42 model built, beginning in 1943 (*upper left*), which were restricted to the main-line tracks in the east. The engine in this photo was captured by U.S. Third Army at Darmstadt on March 25, 1945. The standard Class 52, the first one of which (*lower left*) was built in 1942, was light enough to work virtually all secondary and branchline track in Eastern Europe. There were 6,576 of these locomotives erected by Henschel, Borsig-AEG, Kraus-Maffei, and MBA in Germany, as well as Skoda in Czechoslovakia and Chrzknow in Poland. At the peak of production of Class 52 locomotives in August, 1943, about forty of them (*below*) representing one day's production at one of the giant factories, were being steamed up, ready for delivery. Henschel also produced 176 condenser models of the 52 Class for use in areas of Russia where good water was scarce. Serviced by a huge tender that continually recirculated the used locomotive steam (*above*), one of these engines was capable of operating 700 miles on just 3,500 gallons of water —about 20 times the distance of a standard Class 52 machine!

Bundesarchiv

Wartime Train Movements in Berlin

During a Christmas season early in the war, German soldiers on board a train in Anhalter Station, Berlin (*left*) were bidding farewell to guards on the platform as they departed for leave with their families. In the summer of 1943, there were still smiles on the faces of apparently well-fed civilians (*above*) as they waved to friends who were being evacuated by train to the country, as the Allied aerial offensive began to increase. The odds in the furious battles waged between the armadas of four-motor Anglo-American bombers and the defenders of Germany were symbolized by the battery of two-centimeter flak guns (*below*) mounted on a railway car and silhouetted against an overcast sky from which millions of tons of steel and explosives rained down on the cities of the Reich. Entire trains of antiaircraft guns, delivering tremendous firepower, were moved from one area to another, as Allied target priorities shifted in the campaign to destroy the will of the German nation to wage war.

Two photos, Bundesarchiv

200

Fortresses over Fortress Europe

Perhaps the most famous combat aircraft ever built was the U.S. Army Air Force B-17 Flying Fortress, which gained its greatest renown as being the principal aircraft of the air raids that destroyed the industrial capacity of Germany. The "Forts" assembled in tightly packed formations that could stretch over an area 100 miles long, 10 miles wide, and a mile deep. Of the 12,731 built, about 4,750, each with a 10-man crew, were lost in combat. Individual B-17's—parts of vast formations— are shown over railway targets at Memmingen (*left*) on February 22, 1945 and Kitzingen (*right*) the following day, during the final phases of the strategic bombing campaign. Suffering the fate of hundreds of her sisters, a B-17 is shown exploding in a ball of fire (*above*) during a bomb run over the railroad yards of Nis, Yugoslavia, in April, 1944.

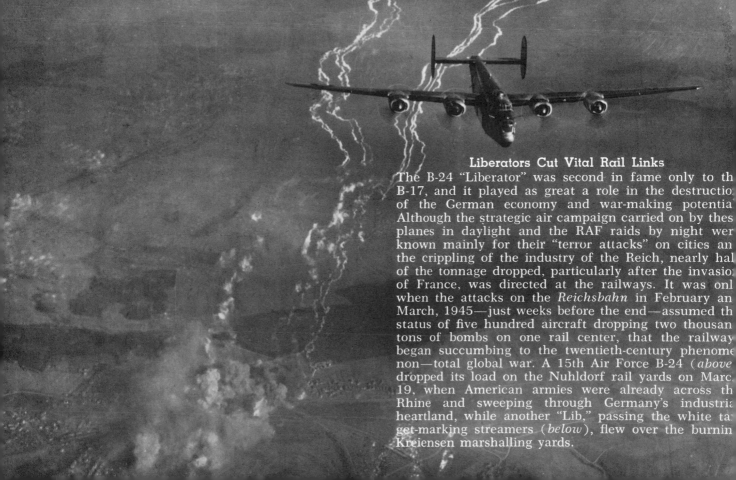

Liberators Cut Vital Rail Links

The B-24 "Liberator" was second in fame only to th B-17, and it played as great a role in the destructio of the German economy and war-making potentia Although the strategic air campaign carried on by thes planes in daylight and the RAF raids by night wer known mainly for their "terror attacks" on cities an the crippling of the industry of the Reich, nearly hal of the tonnage dropped, particularly after the invasio of France, was directed at the railways. It was onl when the attacks on the *Reichsbahn* in February an March, 1945—just weeks before the end—assumed th status of five hundred aircraft dropping two thousan tons of bombs on one rail center, that the railway began succumbing to the twentieth-century phenome non—total global war. A 15th Air Force B-24 (*above* dropped its load on the Nuhldorf rail yards on Marc 19, when American armies were already across th Rhine and sweeping through Germany's industri: heartland, while another "Lib," passing the white ta get-marking streamers (*below*), flew over the burnin Kreiensen marshalling yards.

Ton-Miles Become Bomb-Miles

As the strategic bombing campaign was concluded, the *Reichsbahn* could no longer move freight by the ton-mile; rather it had to measure its resources by the number of bomb hits per mile. Three Liberators (*above*), part of a force of a thousand B-17's and B-24's and four hundred escorting fighters, dropped their bombs on the marshalling yards at Rheine, one of three railway targets of the overwhelming armada. A roundhouse showed clearly under the wingtip of a 15th Air Force B-24 (*below*) as it left the smoking rail junction of Nyiregyhaza, Hungary, September 6, 1944.

Total Envelopment

It may be said that through her early victories Germany sowed the winds of World War II. In 1944 and 1945 she reaped the whirlwind of the

furious assault of her enemies, who closed in from all directions on the ground as well as in the air. There was, within the vast area still controlled by Nazi Germany, literally no place to escape the Allied ground and aerial offensives after the winter of 1943-44. One immediate problem was the pitiful streams of human misery as millions of refugees in the east fled before the armored spearheads and artillery offensives of the Russian Army and the crumbling German fronts left Eastern Europe to the fate of Communist domination. Half-starved, their few belongings partially camouflaged from aerial observation by German Army tent sections and tree branches, Hungarian civilians, soldiers, and a policeman (*above*) slumped exhaustedly on a flatcar on their way to Germany and, hopefully, eventual surrender to the Western Allies poised on the Rhine. Also in Hungary as the Red Army neared, a German soldier (*left*) wearily stood by a flak gun guarding the rear of a train. Meanwhile, fighter-bombers and medium bombers of the 9th U.S. Air Force were joining the B-17 and B-24 attacks on the German rail lines of the interior. The yards at Freiburg were of vital importance to the Germans, since they were the main facility for the dispatching of trains in southwestern Germany. Repeatedly hit, the yards were always put back into service by thousands of laborers. Finally the 9th dealt the Freiburg yards a devastating blow (*upper left*) in support of the ground assault that captured the city shortly afterward. The main depot at Cologne (*right*) was located on one of the most vital transport arteries in Germany, including the bridges over which much of the western front was supplied. The immediate area was the target of sixteen attacks by the 8th Air Force, plus artillery and small arms fire, as ground forces overran the famous city on the Rhine.

Two photos, Bundesarchiv

Two photos, USAF

The Liberation of Belgium

Allied forces swept into Belgium in the autumn of 1944 with the immediate objective of reopening the great port of Antwerp as a huge unloading and staging area from which the railways would haul supplies to the Rhine for stockpiling, preparatory to the final offensive into the heart of Germany early the following spring. The drive went according to plan, and by October 9 American railway troops (*above*) were sharing their cigarettes with their Belgian conductor and two *gendarmes* as they worked their GI 2-8-0 in the Liège yards. On November 17, 1944, an American Army ammunition train (*upper right*) pulled into a railhead near Eupen, within range of German artillery. A month later the last German offensive of the war

smashed into the Ardennes, just fifteen miles south of there and advanced sixty miles westward. Many Military Railway Service personnel were sent to fight as infantry, while others, particularly the 712th, 732nd, and 718th Railway Operating Battalions, ran the trains that helped to turn the tide in the Battle of the Bulge. An official commendation from the headquarters of Patton's Third Army said: " . . . the 732nd was operating railheads literally up to the front line. On occasions the artillery ammunition was delivered by rail right to the guns without the necessity of trucking up from railheads." The 718th ROB at this time accomplished the amazing feat of moving four entire divisions of the Third Army and one

division of the Seventh Army laterally across the front, to close the south flank of the German advance, all within forty-eight hours, under enemy artillery and strafing attacks. By January, 1945, the 743rd ROB was handling all railway activities (*right*) in the port of Antwerp. When a motorized track car carrying a payroll collided head-on with a GI locomotive on a bridge in Belgium, the pay officer had the engine crew spend an hour in a gully, gathering up thousands of dollars in military scrip. After the MRS men handed over the money, the officer pulled his .45 and made the men empty their pockets. Above their vociferous protests, he took every cent, finding when he got back to his own unit that he had several dollars more than before the accident!

Three photos, U.S. Army

Explosive Coal

A favorite booby trap used by retreating German forces was to take coal briquettes, such as those used in engine No. 2317 (*upper left*) switching in the 744th's yard at Charleroi, Belgium, and hollow them out. Such briquettes were filled with explosives and sealed, then thrown on a pile of harmless engine fuel. A few days later, when the Allies were running the facility, an explosion would blow the firebox of a locomotive, killing the crew. MRS men soon learned to break every briquette open, and at least one locomotive returned from a run with two German demolition charges in the cab, where the fireman had gingerly placed them! U.S. Army railroaders refurbished an old Belgian shunter (*lower left*) to switch the port facilities at Ghent. Seventeen MRS men who had been killed in action were honored at ceremonies (*above*) dedicating locomotives to their memories, at Liège on February 27, 1945. Brigadier General Carl R. Gray (*right*), director-general of the MRS, greeted two railway soldiers from his home town. The Antwerp headquarters of the 707th Railway Grand Division (*below*), sponsored by the Southern Railway, was heavily damaged by a V-1 robot bomb.

Four photos, U.S. Army

Southern Railway

U.S. Army photo from AAR

Crossing the Rhine

Once the Siegfried Line, or West Wall, was breached by Allied forces in late 1944 and early 1945, the great natural barrier of the Rhine River was the last obstacle in the west preventing Germany from being overrun. Elaborate plans were being made to establish bridgeheads for crossings, hopefully by mid-April, 1945, when an incredible event shortened the war by six weeks. On the afternoon of March 7 an American reconnaissance company reached the village of Remagen on the west bank of the Rhine, and to their amazement the U.S. soldiers saw the Ludendorff railroad bridge still intact, with hundreds of German civilians and military personnel crossing toward the east. On the opposite side, on the north-south mainline, several locomotives were under steam. In spite of demolitions placed by the Germans and an early temptation by the Americans to destroy the span, it was captured after several hours of heavy fighting. At the height of the assault on the Remagen bridge, a train came chugging along the east bank. The commander of a U.S. armored battalion saw the train, and exclaiming, "Hallelujah! I've always wanted to fire a tank at a locomotive!", he ordered his men to open fire. The engine exploded, the train ground to a halt, and German reinforcements poured out and took up positions in a vain attempt to repel the Americans from the bridge. As five divisions crossed the bridge, much railway equipment was moved up and First Army was advancing one hundred miles beyond the Rhine, confident of a steady stream of supplies by rail. On March 17, however, just four hours after the photo (*above*) was taken, the Ludendorff bridge collapsed, but fifty-five other Rhine bridges, six of them for railroad tracks, were planned by the Army Engineers and some were rushed to completion in time to fill the void left by the loss of the most strategic bridge of the war. One was erected across the Rhine at Wesel, about one hundred miles north of Remagen. Named for Major

Donald P. Kane

Robert Gouldin, an Engineer officer killed during its construction, the 1,752-foot structure was built in just ten days. On April 10 the first train, with Nick Lutseck of the 720th ROB at the throttle (*right*) crossed the Rhine. By the time of the final surrender, 27 days later, 700,000 tons of freight had crossed this dubious-appearing structure. At Mainz news of the death of President Roosevelt came during the nine and a half days of constructing a Rhine bridge, which was named in his honor. A *Reischsbahn* 42 Class engine, hastily lettered "Allied Transportation Corps" is seen (*left*) crossing the FDR Bridge. It was one of almost 3,000 locomotives and 30,000 cars captured in western Germany.

Two photos, U.S. Army

Where Once the Great Formations Flew

It was only after the victorious Allied armies finally overran Germany in the spring of 1945 that the totality of the destruction of *Reichsbahn* facilities became evident. Although the Germans had cleared much of the debris, they could not keep up with the fury of the aerial offensive and all Germany had become a vast railway scrap heap. Locomotives in bomb craters were a common sight, and the collapsed roundhouse at Neustadt (*upper right*) covered several 52 Class war engines. The most famous locomotive mishap of the war occurred at Muenster (*lower right*) when a near miss by a heavy demolition bomb threw a locomotive into the air. It remained coupled to its tender, and the two units formed this crude arch. A British tankman stood at the point of impact, surveying the damage. Although the Germans had filled in the crater and laid a new track, they preferred not to disturb this delicately balanced monument to Allied precision bombing.

Destroy—Then Rebuild

In early May, 1945—a few days before the Germans surrendered on May 7—one of the last raids of the 9th Air Force (*left*) destroyed the yards and two roundhouses at Leipzig. On March 9 over one thousand American four-engine bombers hit the sprawling Henschel foundries at Kassel, and as a result the Germans abandoned their chief source of eighty-eight millimeter guns, tanks, and Class 52 locomotives, one of which (*upper left*) was found, intact and undamaged in the rubble, by American ground forces. The U.S. 757th Railway Shop Battalion took over the Henschel factories and soon had requisitioned enough replacement machinery to put four thousand former Henschel employees to work in eight railway manufacturing plants. To the surprise of the 757th, substantial quantities of completely fabricated subassemblies for Class 52 condenser engines (p. 197) were found at Kassel, and by the end of May the Americans were turning out examples of Germany's "secret railroad weapon." Advancing on Salzburg, Austria, the 20th Armored Division found all bridges except one rail structure destroyed, so they removed the tracks (*above*) to take their tanks across on May 4, 1945. The locomotive on the bridge had been run into a bomb crater by the fleeing Germans. A blown switch frog (*below*) was typical German practice if there was no time to tear up the entire track.

Two photos, National Archives

Seizing the Railway Guns

When British forces arrived at the ammunition dump at Muenster, they found several heavy Italian railway guns (*above*), which had not seen service for a considerable time, camouflaged on a siding nearby. Medium-size guns similar to those that reinforced the Siegfried Line early in the war (p. 22) were inspected by a Canadian soldier (*below*) armed with a British Sten Gun.

Captured Freight of Vast Implications

The final rout of the German Army was so rapid and complete that there was no time for them to destroy even the most confidential, and in terms of future implications the most important, weapons of the war—the V-1 jet robot bombs and the V-2 rockets. When the factory that produced the V-1's was captured, a partially damaged trainload of these rockets (*right*) was found in the vicinity. Fortunately for the Western Allies, the American First Army reached Bromskirchen on March 3, capturing an undamaged trainload of 250-mile-range V-2's (*below*) of the same type that had been directed against England since the previous September. There were enough V-2 parts on or near the train to build almost a hundred of the missiles. They were carefully disassembled, crated, and sent by rail to Antwerp, then shipped to the United States. Dr. Wernher Von Braun, the brilliant young rocket scientist, and many of his staff who had developed the first strategic rocket weapon and made it operational also came to America. Using the V-2's captured by chance in the final offensive of the European war, the United States, supervised by former enemy Von Braun, launched its rocket program, which eventually resulted in the great missile complexes that were to rule (or rule out) future global conflicts. Amer-

Imperial War Museum

ican spacemen who first walked on the moon in 1969 were unwittingly assisted by the soldier guarding that important train with his .50-caliber machine gun at Bromskirchen, twenty-four years earlier.

UPI

Engines in the Orchard

If aerial bombardment caused interesting instances of locomotive demolition, the creative genius of the retreating German railway battalions rendered them a class of Michelangelos of Mayhem. As cited elsewhere in this volume, even the characteristic Teutonic thoroughness and planning sometimes went awry. One of the standard methods of crippling a steam engine was to blow the cylinders with TNT. Usually the right cylinders were demolished and, if time permitted, the left ones as well. There was at least one instance in France when the right cylinders of thirty locomotives in one terminal were methodically blown, while a few miles away, with equal precision, the left cylinders of twenty-five locomotives of the same class were destroyed. Within a few days American railway troops had switched cylinders and had twenty-five operating engines. If there was a lot of explosive to go around, engines were blown literally in half, or their fireboxes or front ends completely demolished. By placing a relatively light charge on the frame, the three main components—boiler, frame, and running gear— could be rendered useless, as was the case of a 2-10-0 (*below*) at Kassel. Other favored methods were not so original, such as crashing two locomotives head-on at high speed, or rolling a dozen engines onto a bridge before dynamiting it. Some enterprising Germans, favoring variety in their wrecks, coupled a dead 2-8-0 and 4-6-0 behind a very live 2-10-0. After pulling the throttle all the way out, they jumped off the big 2-10-0 and let it career toward advancing Allied troops. When the juggernaut hit a particularly sharp curve, all three engines flipped over. The lead squad of Americans, arriving immediately after the wreck occurred (*left*), were accompanied by a photographer in the orchard turned engine yard. In addition to the exploding coal left by the Germans, Allied railway men had to contend with sabotage behind their lines. Occasionally locomotives were stolen and rammed into ammunition or gasoline trains. One saboteur at Erbach let a passenger train run full steam over a demolished bridge, where the wreckage blocked a vital supply road leading to the front. On April 26, 1945, British infantrymen (*lower left*) advanced under heavy fire through the railway yards in Bremen.

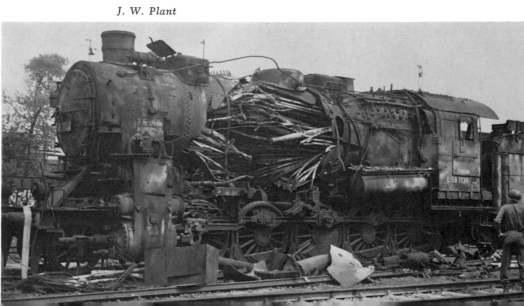

Abandoned Equipment

A German ten-wheeler, its main rods removed so that the engine could be hauled dead, was artfully camouflaged, including a pine tree in the stack. Near Langenprezelten (*below*) U.S. forces captured one of the flak trains, which failed to halt the aerial offensive. A trainload of *Luftwaffe* Ju-88 aircraft (*lower right*) was guarded by a U.S. flak battery after its capture near the "Pied Piper" village of Hamelin.

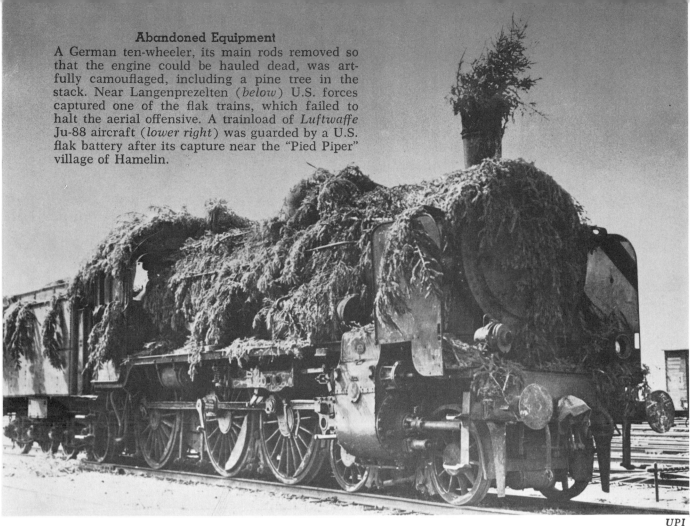

Human Freight

During the advance through France and the Low Countries, most trains returning from the front consisted of long strings of empties. Once in Germany, however, all manner of human freight was carried back in the boxcars and gondolas of the MRS. The liberation of thousands of French, Dutch, and Belgian workers in the industrial areas, tens of thousands of Allied prisoners of war, and inmates of concentration camps added a tremendous burden to the job of the military railroaders. As soon as the hundreds of thousands of displaced persons—DP's—were freed, they wanted to get home immediately. There had also been POW trains bringing in captured Germans in France, but nothing like the tens—and at the end—hundreds—of thousands of prisoners who were bagged daily by the Allied armies. German prisoners had always been carried in boxcars, but with the flood of humanity surging westward, there often were no boxcars available for POW moves. In such instances the prisoners were loaded in open gondolas and a guard armed with a Thompson submachine gun was assigned to each car. Some of these POW train movements did not add to the laurels of the U.S. Army in general, or the Military Railway Service in particular. There were no sanitary facilities aboard these freight cars, and even late in the war many Germans did not feel defeated at all, so it was most advisable for Allied soldiers to stand clear of passing POW trains! On one particularly hot day a trainload of POW's halted at a French station to water the locomotive. The Germans in the open gondola cars who had not had a drink all day, began calling for water. By the time the train was ready to pull out, a loud chorus of "Wasser, Wasser" was raised from each car. The locomotive began to pull out slowly, and the fireman merely left the water column turned on to its full capacity of a thousand gallons a minute, right over the track. The Germans,

drenched and standing in water and filth up to their waists, were furious. Some of the military police who guarded the prisoners actually committed atrocities, but were never brought to account for their deeds. In direct violation of the Geneva Convention, POW's were sealed in boxcars and the airvents covered, in some early prison train movements in France. After scores of them suffocated, particularly in tunnels, the practice was halted. There were acts of brutality, as one MRS veteran recalls. He was a block operator at a small station when a POW train pulled in. An Army truck had arrived with rations for the prisoners and two POW's from each car were to get the food for the other fifty or so men jammed into the small French "40 and 8's" (forty men or eight horses). Usually there were at least two or three men in each car who understood English, but when an MP began shouting the orders into one carload of Germans, they were all confused—none could understand. Suddenly the MP grabbed a particularly small German, yanked him out of the car, broke his jaw, kicked him, and beat him with his tommy-gun butt. When the MRS operator tried to intervene, the MP leveled the gun at him. After that the operator always carried a weapon of his own, but never experienced a comparable situation again. Prisoners were trouble for both sides. There is a story that one American airman who was shot down over Germany had not been well searched by his captors and still carried a pack of cigarettes and matches. While being held at a railroad station, he was allowed to use the men's toilet, incredibly without an escort. A slow-moving ammunition train was rolling by directly outside the window of the washroom, so the airman hastily lit a cigarette, took a few puffs, closed the match book around the unlit end and flipped this spur-of-the-moment time-delay incendiary through an open boxcar door. A few miles outside of town, the whole train is said to have exploded.

USAF

Liberating the Death Camps

When American troops of the 157th Infantry Regiment arrived at Dachau, Germany, on April 30, 1945, it was under fire and their immediate task (*right*) was to ferret out the SS guards at the concentration camp. At the moment that this combat photo was made, the men had no idea of the contents of the high-side gondola cars spotted among the trees in the background. They soon found out. Hitler's "final solution to the Jewish problem" (and other ethnic "problems") was indeed final. Concentration camps were established at various isolated locations in Germany and the occupied countries. Then Jews, gypsies, and other "undesirable social elements" were relentlessly hunted down, packed into sealed boxcars, and carried to the concentration camps where they were systematically exterminated. Unfortunately the *Reichsbahn* was the means used for virtually all of these woebegone movements. It was the job of Colonel Adolph Eichmann, who was later tried and executed by the State of Israel for his role in the administration of this policy, to organize the secret train movements that carried an estimated six million civilians—one way—to the camps, a fact that, when presented as evidence, weighed heavily in the outcome of the trial. The train that the American soldiers fought near and others spotted nearby, contained the bodies of hundreds of victims, most of whom had starved to death en route to Dachau. These trains were among the first tangible discoveries to confirm the horrendous stories that had been coming out of Hitler's Europe for years, and the trains shown here received worldwide notoriety almost immediately. Soon the mass graves, the cremation ovens, and the experiences of the pitiable survivors were also re-

vealed to a world that, though accustomed to the senseless atrocities of a vicious war, recoiled from this ultimate horror. With the connivance of pro-Axis elements in occupied countries, and in the case of Russia, the tacit approval of Stalin, who did nothing to try to save two million Russian Jews, a majority of European Jews had been shot, starved, and gassed by the Nazis. Within hours of the liberation of Dachau, U.S. Army Signal Corps photographers (*below left*) recorded the wretched remnants of Nazi racial theories on the railroad tracks of the camp. Young members of

the *Hitlerjugend*—the Nazi youth movement—some of whom had been snipers against U.S. troops, were forced to view the contents of the cars (*below center*) at Dachau. Some idea of the movement of people associated with the camps is shown (*lower right*) at the infamous Buchenwald facility. Three surviving Jewish youths, from Poland, Latvia, and Hungary, displayed a homemade Israeli flag as they prepared to leave Europe for the last time by rail, to begin anew by building a nation in Palestine. Although atrocities were committed by all of the belligerents in World War II, only in

the case of the Axis and Communist Russia were they routine government policy. Acts of bestiality on the part of the Allies, such as those recorded elsewhere in this volume, were usually isolated cases of local military commanders or individuals who violated the laws of their own armies. There was also the forced repatriation of Soviet citizens after the cessation of hostilities, an incredibly stupid and naive decision by the President of the United States, who probably had no idea of the terrible fate that was to befall the victims of his ill-considered concessions to Stalin.

Four photos, U.S. Army

Two photos, U.S. Army

Two photos, U.S. Army from Railroad Magazine

Why Railroad Soldiers Cursed the Work of Their Own Air Force

In April, 1945, a track crew of the U.S. 746th Railway Operating Battalion (*below*) began opening the first track through the bombed-out passenger yard at Marburg, while in the nearby roundhouse (*above*) members of the 757th Railway Shop Battalion worked on the superheater unit of one of the seventeen German engines that they returned to service in the first four days of their occupation of the facility. Fifteenth Air Force bombs tossed locomotives around like toys (*upper left*) in the engine terminal at Linz, Austria. Two crewmen from the 712th ROB (*left*) are shown as they adjusted a valve on a camouflaged German 2-8-2.

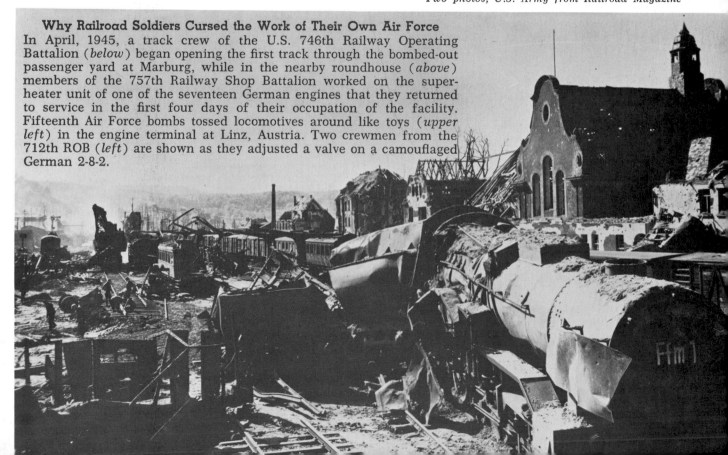

Temporary Bridges and Momentary Hazards

In a last futile attempt to slow the Allies, German demolition teams tried to destroy every bridge that had not been hit from the air, such as the one (*right*) near Torgau, where American and Russian troops finally linked forces on the Elbe River on April 25, 1945. Temporary spans were erected at Herzogenrath (*below*) and at Aschaffenberg (*lower right*). Most of these hastily erected military bridges were as flimsy as they looked. They were never intended to last beyond the time required to fulfill their immediate military mission and were replaced by more permanent structures as soon as the military situation, labor, and materials permitted. At Nuremberg the headquarters of "C" Company, 728th ROB, was a GI caboose (*bottom right*) in 1945. James R. Boerckel, a Long Island Rail Road man who spent most of the war with the 733rd, recalls that European railroading, especially the practice of no headlights on locomotives, was alien to American railway men, but under wartime restrictions of complete blackout, running on an unfamiliar line that could have any number of physical impairments—bomb or shell craters, damaged bridges, sabotage—it could be a nerve-racking experience. Besides the standard flagging equipment of lanterns and red flag, a carbine was often carried, since a train was not the only thing that might have to be stopped dead in its tracks! For day signals the 733rd used German stop boards during that last winter of the war. They had to be installed rapidly, and if the ground was frozen, a few carbine slugs loosened up the dirt. At Hochspeyer, Boerckel had to plant one of these boards, mounted on a metal spike, right in the asphalt station platform. Stepping behind a packing crate with a German MP-40 *Schmeisser* submachine gun, he emptied a magazine into the platform, leaving an ample hole for the stop board. It is said that one enterprising railroader welded a metal bracket on the side of a GI tender, bolted a *Schmeisser* to the bracket, and whenever he needed a hole along the right of way for any purpose, he positioned the locomotive in the proper location, inserted a magazine in the gun, looped a lanyard around the trigger, ducked into the coal bunker, and fired away. After a while the engine cab and tender looked as if they had been strafed —having taken many of the ricochets that spewed in all directions. Even after the shooting stopped and the *Luftwaffe* no longer attacked their trains, railway troops faced dangerous hazards. There were hundreds of unexploded bombs and dud demolition charges that could be very temperamental, especially if disturbed by a wrecking crane or rails being dragged over the ground. There were also plenty of unused munitions scattered about, from nine-millimeter ammunition to V-1's. Several men of the 733rd were cleaning out some boxcars when they discovered crates of *Panzerfaust* antitank rocket launchers. When they threw the weapons out of the car, one ignited and the rocket took off right down the track and blew up a boxcar that was unoccupied at the time.

U.S. Army

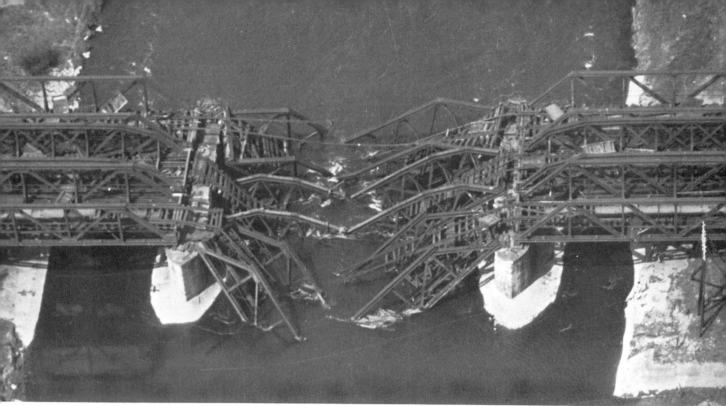

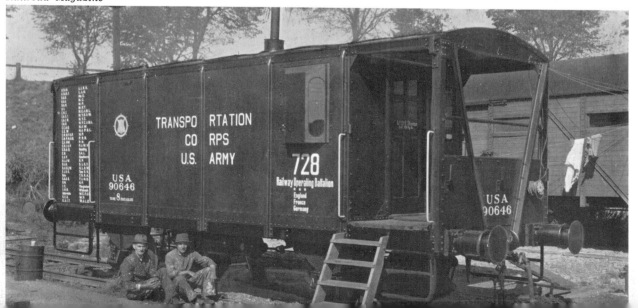

Unconditional Surrender

The facts of the complete defeat of Germany during the Second World War were evident throughout the former Third Reich. Wartime field engines, such as No. 42-1007 (*left*) at Hanau, were being operated by soldiers of the conquering armies. Bridges that had been destroyed by American bombers were repaired by American engineers, and American locomotives operated over them (*below left*) in places like Stolberg. In all, the United States had contributed the greatest share of any nation to the final victory. In addition to the millions of articles of military hardware, over 8,000 locomotives and 103,000 freight cars were exported from the United States, the vast majority of this equipment going to the European theater. By June 11, 1945, a semblance of normalcy began returning to the shattered *Reichsbahn* when the first train to Hanover (*right*) operated by German civilians and the 722nd, which was sponsored by the Seaboard Air Line Railroad, prepared to leave Bremerhaven. By and large, the Americans had found the German railway workers the easiest civilians to work with. Unlike the liberated French, the Germans, who were accustomed to accepting authority, recognized the finality of their defeat. As an ultimate expression of total Allied victory and control of the German railways, the pride of the *Reichsbahn*, a high-speed streamlined passenger locomotive (*below*) that had often sped top Nazi

W. E. Lawhorne

dignitaries to their appointments with destiny, was set upon by several former employees of the Atlantic Coast Line Railroad, who applied the official emblem of that railway to the front of the proudest locomotive of a vanquished enemy.

Earl Weed

Rising Sun in the Pacific

Although World War II began in the Far East with the massive Japanese aerial attacks throughout the Central Pacific and Eastern Asia on December 7–10, 1941, the large-scale hostilities leading up to "the Day of Infamy" dated back more than a decade, and the basic causes, almost forty years. Once Japan had defeated Russia in the 1904 war, consolidating her grip on Korea and Formosa and obtaining bases in China, her influence spread steadily eastward. After World War I Japan received former German colonies in the Marshall and Mariana Islands. At precisely the same period the United States, as the new dominant power of the Eastern Pacific, was advancing ever westward. A collision of interests was inevitable. A minor incident at Mukden, China, on September 8, 1931—exactly ten years and three months before Pearl Harbor—sparked a full-scale Japanese invasion of Manchuria. The fighting in China eventually spread across Southeast Asia to India and along a six-thousand-mile arc encompassing Burma, Thailand, Malaya, Indonesia, the Carolines, Marshalls, the Marianas, and almost engulfing Australia, by 1942. The Asian continent, plus Australia and the Philippines, possessed large rail networks of strategic importance. Plantation railways, port switching lines, and even

sugarcane railroads figured in some tactical situations on the lesser, but bloodily fought, islands.

230

Japanese Advance in China

By 1937 Japanese troops had landed in central China from their Formosa base, to advance on the bombed railroad yards of Hankow (*above*), and set up positions on the main Shanghai rail line (*left*). At the Chapei station in northern Shanghai (*below*) Chinese antiaircraft gunners, wearing German and British helmets, whipped out their sidearms to fire futilely on the Japanese planes that destroyed their antiaircraft guns.

"Banzai" on the Railway

A Japanese armored car converted to rail service (*upper left*) is shown in China on May 28, 1938. A rare gem of the armored railcar builder's art, complete with Japanese soldier peering from the hatch above his machinegun (*left*) was guarding a train near Chingchow. A Chinese Army heavy armored car, surmounted with two cannon turrets is seen (*below*) shortly after its capture by Japanese troops. As the Japanese thrust toward Kweilin in 1944, principal advance base of the United States 14th Air Force (General Claire L. Chennault's former *"Flying Tigers"*), 100,000 civilians fled the city; 20,000 of them jammed every available running board and car roof (*below right*) of trains heading for safety. In their dash across the provinces of Shansi and Hopei in northern China, Japanese troops (*above*) raised their rifles and flags in a rousing "banzai" cheer near Niengtsekwang on November 11, 1937.

Photoworld

Two photos, National Archives

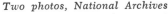

"... the steam engine altered the proportions of th
globe, ... ships arrived ... and knocked at the well
barred feudal doors of Japan with weapons and ideas.
—Winston Churchil

The rapid advance of Imperial Japan
from a feudal society that had n
concept of industry, power politics
or modern weaponry, into the undis
puted master of the entire Western
Pacific and temporary victor over th
greatest power the world had eve
seen, in little over eighty years
amazed Hitler as much as it di
Roosevelt and Churchill. But this up
heaval was not without flaws, which
were to prove disastrous to the bri
liant Japanese nation. As the fifth
decade of the twentieth century ap
proached, however, Japan, like he
future Axis allies in Europe, knew
only victory in each succeeding bol
military venture. In the long China
campaign, railways were of crucia
importance, with the Japanese rap
idly restoring service as quickly a
they advanced. Upon finding tha
Japanese soldiers paid cash for thei
wares, Chinese merchants (*uppe
left*) met all trains carrying troops t
the front. At Pukow in 1938, Japa
nese railway troops (*left*) decked out
Chinese locomotive with their flags
Both the power of Japan and th
artistry of her military photogra
phers were evident in this scen
(*above*) of Japanese infantry wit
their battle flag on an American-buil
Shay locomotive. While one o
Chiang Kai-shek's soldiers sat on th
pilot beam, a locomotive took wate
(*upper right*) at Ho-keou. Two Jap
anese sentries (*right*) patrolled th
tracks by their bunker on a Shang
hai rail line.

India Holds the Line

When Great Britain declared war on Germany on September 3, 1939, she brought the entire resources of her vast empire into the conflict. One of her greatest assets was India, which formed the anchor of the South Pacific defense line against the Japanese and provided tough, bold, and seasoned combat troops, which fought alongside British "Tommies" in every theater. They also provided railway construction and operating units, which saw widespread service in the China-Burma-India sector as well as in the Middle East, Africa, and Italy. Fearing a Japanese invasion from French Indochina through Burma and Thailand, India rushed to reinforce her eastern frontiers. In March, 1941, troops deployed in the Keren Hills on the Burma frontier received their supplies directly by rail. In the early light of dawn (*right*) the morning train was loaded with rations, water, ammunition, and sandbags. A carload of barbed wire concertina, lubricants, and water (*lower right*) was being inspected by British soldiers prior to being unloaded at the supply dump in the Keren Hills. The armed forces of India assembled a trainload of equipment, which toured the nation and informed the populace as to the varied means of defending them. The Defence Forces Exhibition Train, complete with a fighter aircraft mock-up and a destroyer gun turret and mast and decorated with Indian sailors (*below*), was photographed at Lahore in October, 1941. When the Japanese did attempt a full-scale invasion of India in 1944, air-conditioned ambulance trains carried wounded troops to the rear. Recuperating Indian soldiers (*left*) are shown peering from one of the hospital cars on the line from Comilla to Calcutta, en route to rear-area hospitals from the Burma front.

Four photos, Indian Ministry of Defence

Americans Operate the Bengal & Assam

What the Trans-Iranian Railway accomplished in supplying the Russians in the Caucasus region, the Bengal & Assam provided in eastern India for the supply of Chinese forces trying to repel the Japanese and for Allied units in the invasion of Burma. The B & A however, was much less secure, and during the Japanese assault on India in the spring of 1944 the rail lifeline to the Burma front nearly fell under Japanese occupation. In December, 1943, the advance elements of a large MRS force, which ultimately included the 705th Railway Grand Division, the 721st, 725th, 726th, 745th, and 748th Railway Operating Battalions, and the 758th Railway Shop Battalion, arrived to set up headquarters preparatory to taking over the operation of 658 miles of the 738-mile rail supply route from the port of Calcutta to the terminal of the famous Ledo Road on the northern frontier of Burma. In that area of upper Assam Province the air bases were established to fly supplies "over the hump" of the Himalayas to supply the rapidly developing B-29 base complexes that soon brought Japan to the brink of annihilation. The Ledo Road wound south to the Burma Road, where the bulk of supplies moved into China, once it was recaptured from the Japanese. The Bengal & Assam was indeed one of the most vital rail links of the war. One of the principal bottlenecks was the car ferry across the Brahmaputra River. When the MRS took over the line, the ferry handled two hundred cars in each direction daily. Soon that figure was quadrupled, partly because of the installation of floodlights for night operations (*left*) at the terminals of Amingoan and Pandau. T/Sergeant Charles E. Roth (*lower left*) was trying to ignore a sacred cow as he greased a locomotive. One of the 262 Lend-lease locomotives (*below*) sent to augment the B & A roster of 713 engines is shown in 1944.

Three photos, U.S. Army

Five photos, U.S. Army

Indian Allies and U.S. Army Operations

When the American Military railroaders arrived in India, they found that the British had already recruited experienced railway men for military service in similar fashion to that of the MRS. In all, there were no fewer than ninety-eight companies of Indian military railway troops, plus various headquarters and sections, most of them operating on the Burma front. As in most instances, the U.S. Military Railway Service utilized the existing civilian workers as much as possible. The rail terminal at Ledo (*above*) was mile 0.00 of the Ledo Road. From here the trucks had 1,074 miles of mountains, jungles, and Japanese to

Kunming, China. Indian women were employed at Gauhati (*left*) to clean the fires of 726th ROB locomotives. Engines were coaled in a most primitive manner (*upper right*) in the 748th ROB yard in Tinsukia. At Mariani, where the sectors of the 745th and 748th ROB's met (*right center*), the local populace watched a movie camera crew recording the antics of B & A engine No. 180, where Japanese troops had been less than five miles away just a few months previously. Elephants were useful in the role of switch engines, as the eighty-year-old specimen named "Moonbeam" (*right*) at Bogapani demonstrates. Since elephants were vital to the local economy and performed useful wartime functions, they were often transported by railway in special elephant cars. One day an American engineer was amazed to find that his locomotive was dangerously low on water, even though the tender had just been filled. When he went back to check the level in the tank, he was flabbergasted to find that an elephant, the cargo of the first car in the train, had opened the water hatch and had been ecstatically giving himself a prolonged shower! In spite of the difficulties involved in operating the Bengal & Assam Railway, which included having to rebuild much of the line, fighting off Japanese marauders, great difficulty in communication with native workers and the presence of three different track gauges along the line, the MRS managed to move over 6.2 million tons of freight and 5,559 passenger trains from February, 1944, until the line was returned to civilian control shortly after V-J Day in September, 1945.

Indian Ministry of Defence

Two photos, USAF

Tree-Top Tactics

Because of the lack of good roads, the Japanese forces in Southeast Asia had to rely on the railways for their main overland distribution supply lines. The Anglo-American air units based in the area developed nerve-racking (to aircrews and enemy alike) tactics of screaming in at tree-top level to strafe and bomb the rail lines. First fighters, then medium bombers and even heavy bombers, employed these tactics with great success, sometimes returning with palm branches, bird nests, and even pieces of enemy equipment, uniforms, and soldiers in their air scoops and gunports. American B-24's of the 7th Bombardment Group hit the bridge spanning the Mae Khlong River (*left*), near the fork with the Kwai River in Thailand. When it was found that bombs frequently bounced off railway tracks, the 10th U.S. Air Force developed spiked bombs (*below*), which stuck in the roadbed where they hit. Royal Air Force Hurricanes and Beaufighters caught Japanese trains at Sakantra (*lower left*), and at a point on the Mandalay-Rangoon line (*lower right*), as well as an unidentified point on the Burma plains (*right*). In the two latter photos cannon fire has also hit the tenders, causing water to cascade from the tanks.

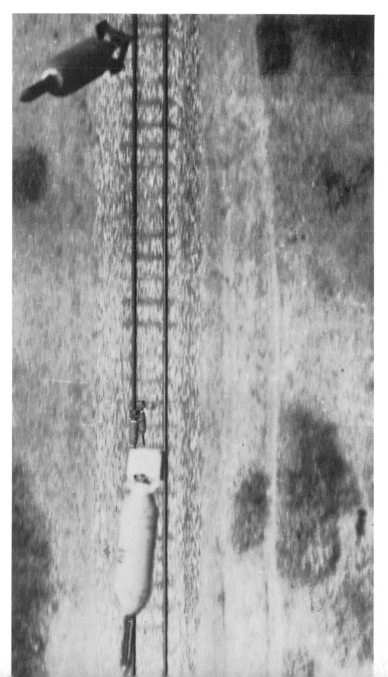

The Railway of Death

Of all the tragic railway ventures of World War II, one stands out as being perhaps the most costly in terms of human suffering, the most forgotten in the annals of history, and yet it inspired one of the most famous dramas of that era. When the Japanese consolidated their grip on Southeast Asia in 1942, they began construction of a railway line from Bangkok, Thailand, northwest along the Kwai River, across the virtually uninhabited Bilauktaung Mountains, along the Andaman seacoast, and up to Moulmein, Burma, and a connection with the line to Rangoon. Allied estimates place the death toll among the forced laborers on the Burma-Thailand Railway—from disease, brutality, and starvation—as high as 300,000 civilians and 11,000 Allied prisoners of war. Steep grades, deep cuts (*left*) and spindly trestles, such as the Hintok-Tampie Bridge (*right*), which could have been a prototype for *The Bridge over the River Kwai*, were typical of the engineering feats performed in just a year of construction, plus much rebuilding of the three-hundred-mile line that fell under constant Allied aerial bombardment. Immediately after the Japanese surrender, when these photos were taken, over five thousand Japanese prisoners were put to work upgrading the line. A crew of them is shown (*lower right*) working on the track near Kanchanaburi, about seventy-five miles west of Bangkok and near the collapsed bridge on the previous pages. Some of the more fortunate coolies (*below*), who survived three years of the appalling conditions on the "Death Valley Railway," were en route back to their homes in November, 1945. The line still exists as far as Ban Sai Yok in Thailand and Ye in Burma, but over a hundred miles of track in the most rugged border terrain have long since returned to oblivion, the ghost line of the thousands of its victims whose bones lie in shallow graves along its crumbling embankments.

Australian War Memorial

Indian Ministry of Defence

Imperial War Museum

Indian Ministry of Defence

Recapturing the Burmese Railways

It took until the spring of 1945—just months before the end—to turn the tenacious Japanese hold on Burma into rout. On May 3 two members of the Frontier Force Rifles (*above left*) lay prone in the Prome railway yards, firing on a Japanese rear-guard position that offered little resistance to the advancing British troops. In June twenty-five pounder guns, mounted on drop-side gondola cars (*above right*) were hauled by jeep railcars from their base at the rail junction in Nyaunglebin (*below*) to support British Empire forces battling along the railway. These trains were manned jointly by Indian Rajput gunners and British West York Infantry. Jeeps proved to be a practical, versatile, and expendable form of motive power in the Burmese jungles. British colonial forces and the Army used them to great advantage. Near Pinwe an English patrol (*upper right*) used a crude wooden framework as a turntable to reverse the direction of their vehicle, or to move it to a storage track off the main line. Armed with an assortment of weapons, including a Thompson submachine gun, Sten guns, Enfield rifles, and an automatic rifle (*lower right*), Indian troops of the 17th Division moved south from Meiktila toward Rangoon in April. The jeep-locomotive was powerful enough to haul two boxcars loaded with supplies. This railroad line was vital to the advance of the Fourteenth Army on its dash to Rangoon and the recapture of the Malay Peninsula.

Two photos, Indian Ministry of Defence

U.S. Army, from Railroad Magazine

Restoring the Rail Lines

As American and Chinese forces under General Stilwell drove down from the north, British and Indian troops under Admiral Mountbatten's command struck out from India along the Irrawaddy River and the main rail line from Mandalay toward Rangoon. An amphibious assault on Rangoon sent British forces north to meet the southward thrusts at Prome and Pegu. This operation resulted in the liberation of much of Burma and the re-opening of the Burma Road supply line to China. When the Anglo-American thrusts reached Myitkyina in August, 1944, destroyed bridges (*right*), the work of Allied air attacks and retreating Japanese forces, were the rule, and engineer units, such as the Indians (*below*), working south of Pinwe, set to work immediately to restore the vital rail links. The U.S. Army 330th Engineer Battalion completed the Loilaw Bridge (*lower right*), with seven girder spans plus three of the renowned Bailey Bridge truss sections in the center, four miles south of Mogaung, on October 22, 1944.

Three photos, U.S. Army from Railroad Magazine

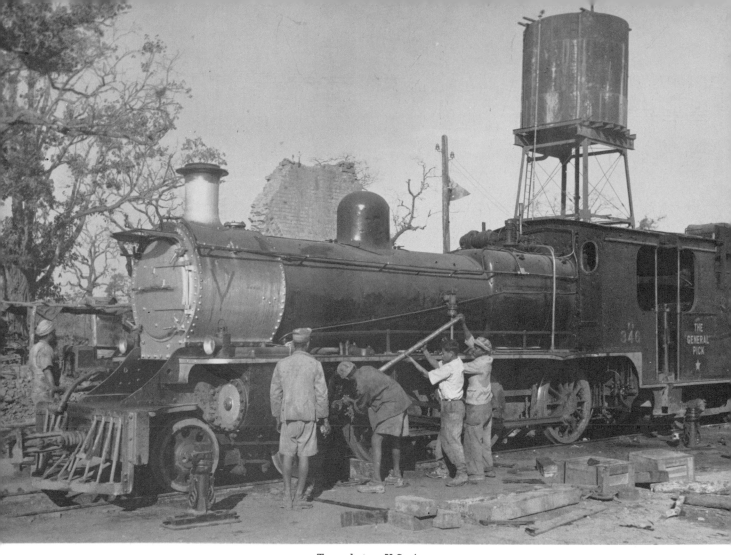

The Railway Effort in the South Pacific

As the Allies recaptured the railways of Burma, rehabilitation progressed rapidly, since the lack of roads made rail the only means of mass overland supply. By January, 1945, the shops at Myitkyina were back in operation, and a trim little 4-6-0 (*above*), a "V" for victory painted on her smokebox, was named in honor of the Ledo Road builder, American Brigadier General Lewis A. Pick (*left*), shown at the throttle of No. 346 on January 10. When General Douglas MacArthur was ordered from the Philippines to Australia before the rapid Japanese advance in 1942, a high-ranking staff of U.S. Military Railway officers arrived at about the same time to lay the groundwork for U.S. operation of the Australian rail system in the event of a Japanese invasion. When the Japanese advance was halted, it became evident that U.S. operation of the railways would not be necessary. The railways of Australia contributed heavily to the war effort, especially since the island continent had become the main staging area for rolling back the Japanese in the South Pacific. An Australian regiment of the 7th Division (*upper right*) was en route to reinforce the 6th Division in the Middle East in October, 1941. The South Australian Railway Workshops turned out all manner of war vehicles (*right*) as well as new locomotives.

Two photos, Australian War Memorial

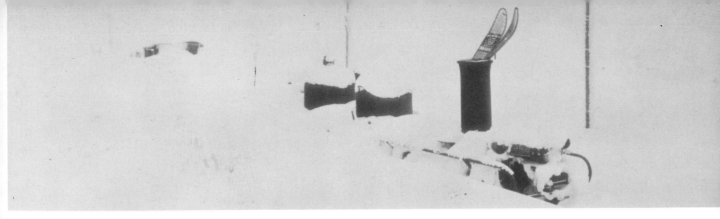

Army Railroading in the Klondike

Even before the Japanese invaded the eastern end of the Aleutian Island chain, the great strategic value of Alaska was recognized by the military authorities. In 1942 the U.S. government leased the narrow-gauge White Pass & Yukon Route, which runs from Skagway to Whitehorse, in the Canadian Yukon. Second-hand locomotives were purchased from the Denver & Rio Grande Western, and new ones were built by Baldwin in 1943, for the tonnage carried by the WP & Y increased *elevenfold* between 1941 and 1943, because of the hauling of construction supplies for the Al-Can Highway and U.S. airbases. This illustrates once again the immense flexibility of rail transport. Meanwhile the government-owned Alaska Railroad was taken over by the 714th ROB, which operated the line for the duration, then returned to Fort Eustis, Virginia, where it remained twenty-five years later as the last active railway unit in the U.S.

Army. The legendary storms of Alaska wreaked their worst on both railroads during the wartime winters. On the WP & Y (*above left, near left,* and *above*) experienced narrow-gauge men from Colorado battled the blizzards. Engine No. 254 (*above*), with the photographer's snowshoes in the stack, came from the D & RGW; three of her identical sisters still pull the famous Silverton Train. An Alaska Railroad rotary plow (*below*) became stuck in the winter of 1943-44. Not all of nature's vendettas came in the winter; the crew of engine No. 702 of the Alaska Railroad narrowly escaped death (*lower left*) when a flash flood swept the bridge near Healy from under their tender in the summer of 1944. The following Christmas, a parlor car on the rear of the Post Exchange train (*far left*) was manned by men of the 714th, who distributed gifts to all the Eskimo children along the Alaska Railroad.

Sunset of the Japanese Empire

Because of the vast expanses of ocean and the virtually impassable jungle and mountain terrain, logistics in the islands campaign, from Australia to Okinawa, were dependent mainly on shipping and air. In sectors of ground fighting, however, railways, no matter how insignificant or primitive, were utilized to the greatest extent. Here the use of field expedients—making do with what's on hand, while top priorities of the Allies went to the European war—so common to the South Pacific, carried into the railroad realm. Narrow-gauge tracks, intended to carry sugar cane to refineries, supplied beleaguered U.S. Marines and Japanese forces on Guadacanal, New Guinea, Tinian, and Saipan. Railways in Australia, New Caledonia, and other areas used as staging points against the Japanese carried many times their prewar tonnages. On Borneo and Angaur Island, little industrial lines were bombed by Allied aircraft prior to their capture. A top priority during the liberation of the Philippines was the activation of rail service, and General MacArthur returned to Manila by rail. In spite of heavy fighting, the Chinese railroads held up, as did the Japanese National Railways, under the heaviest of B-29 attacks. Even in Hiroshima, rail service was restored within thirty-six hours of the atomic attack on August 6, 1945.

Railroad Magazine

U.S. Army
Bill Hounsell

Far-Flung Rail Operations

In 1943 a U.S. Navy officer pounded in the last spike (*left*) of the Guadalcanal, Bougainville & Tokyo line while natives, some of them paramilitary guerrillas, watched. It was to be over two years and 2,500 miles to the last name in the title of the island line. Another view of the scene on page 1 shows what a direct bomb hit did to a locomotive (*above*) in southeastern China in 1945. American Air Force units, landing in Karachi on the Arabian Sea coast of India, faced a rail journey of over two weeks to the advance bases in Assam. One Private Marrow (*right*), of the 13th Ferrying Command, was getting a shave from an Indian barber in the Karachi depot when the train pulled out. Marrow wisely retracted his head when the barber began to run alongside attempting to finish the job. It is not known if the barber was paid for his services.

Two photos, U.S. Army

What the Japanese Left Behind

As Allied forces advanced through the Dutch East Indies and up the Marianas chain, they found many light railways, including locomotives of German manufacture. In the largest railway yard on any isolated Pacific island, troops of the U.S. 81st Division, advancing across Angaur Island, discovered abandoned Japanese engines (*above*) that had been built in Berlin when Germany was a prominent colonial power in the Pacific. More German locomotives were found on a dock at Balikpapan, Borneo (*right*), months after the oil-carrying railway over which the Japanese operated them had been knocked out by the 13th AAF. During the hard-fought battle for Tinian, Marines (*upper right*) paused to rest and do some maintenance work on their little cane car. When a Japanese assault on New Caledonia appeared inevitable, Major General Alexander M. Patch (*left*) inspected a locomotive on April 4, 1942. This locomotive was one of three operating in Nouméa.

USMC photo from Railroad Magazine

USAF

Saipan—Vital Stop on the Road to Tokyo

In June, 1944, Admiral Chester Nimitz brought a huge force of ships and Marines into the Marianas, invading Guam, Tinian, and Saipan with the primary purpose of establishing bases for the ultimate weapon in the assault on the Japanese homeland—the Boeing B-29 Superfortress. Once on Saipan, the Marines quickly seized a light railway that operated between a sugar refinery and Isely Field, which was soon enlarged to accommodate the B-29's. Construction supplies were brought in on the railway even before the Japanese were cleared from the area. A dead Japanese soldier (*right*) lay sprawled near engine No. 8, whose builder's plate reads: *Orenstein & Koppel A.G. Berlin. Sole Agents, Otto Reimers & Co. Tokyo.* By June 26 the Marines had dealt the little 0-4-0T a near-fatal dose of graffiti (*below*) and had unceremoniously disposed of the English-language plate that had been fixed by the German builders onto the Japanese locomotive. The leathernecks, reflecting their origins, had scrawled such phrases as "New York Central," "L. A. Bound," "Kansas Cannon Ball," "The Susie-Q," "The Toonerville Trolley," and "SIRT"* on the flanks of engine and water car. The other operable engine, an 0-6-0T (*left*) is shown being returned to service at the airfield. When a Southerner lettered "South Carolina" on the right side of the little lokie, a Yankee countered with "New York Express" on the left. The little sugar line carried fuel, ammunition, bombs, and parts that maintained the great Superfortress armada as it flew from Saipan to smash the cities, the economy, and the railways of the Japanese islands 1,500 miles to the northwest.

* Staten Island Rapid Transit.

National Archives (USCG)

U.S. Army

U.S. Army

MacArthur Returns—by Train

For months prior to the Allied invasion of the Philippine Islands, American aviators of both the Air Force and Navy carried out furious low-level attacks against the Japanese-operated railways on Luzon. Using parafrag (PARAchute FRAGmentation) bombs (*upper left*), aircraft of the 5th and 13th Air Forces could scream in at treetop level, yet escape the explosions of their own bombs that drifted down by parachute. Sometimes they barely missed getting caught in bomb bursts (*left*). On January 20, 1945, only eleven days after U.S. troops invaded Luzon, heavily armed Americans guarded a Filipino engine (*above*) against frequent Japanese attacks. Shortly after the liberation of Manila, General MacArthur (*below*) addressed the assembled troops, who welcomed the diesel powered *General MacArthur Special*.

Railroad Magazine

To Dagupan, to San Fabian, to San Agustin

Allied forces landed at Leyte, in the Philippines, in October, 1944, the first bloody step across the islands to liberate Luzon and the capital city of Manila. Three months later the overwhelming American fleet steamed into Lingayen Gulf and U.S. forces stormed ashore near Dagupan. Barely two weeks later, trainloads of ammunition (*right*), food, medical supplies, and equipment ran south from Dagupan toward the front, which was drawing ever closer to the capital along the right of way of the Manila Railroad. Hundreds of armed surviving Japanese troops were waging guerrilla warfare behind the Allied lines, so all trains were heavily guarded. San Fabian, just north of Dagupan on the Lingayen Gulf, was shelled by the Navy during the landings. On January 20 Filipino trackmen (*lower right*) repaired tracks at the station that were knocked out by the shelling. Just a few days after the beachhead was established, the first U.S. Army MRS unit, the 790th Railway Operating Company, came ashore and began opening the rail line toward Manila. They found the railroad in deplorable condition, because of Allied bombardment, a virtual absence of maintenance for three years, and sabotage by the retreating Japanese. Once again the inherent flexibility, not only of the railway, but of the steam locomotive, saved the transportation situation. Since absolutely no coal was available to the 790th, they used pulpwood, lumber, old ties, driftwood, and even coconut hulls for engine fuel. The modern strategists who believe that diesel locomotives, with their dependence on oil fuel and regular maintenence, can handle all future combat rail situations have already forgotten the lessons of the Manila Railroad steam locomotives. The railway line from San José to San Agustin, on Mindoro Island, was restored by the 866th Aviation Engineer Battalion (*below*) in December, 1944, to supply forward air bases whose planes were striking at the Japanese on Luzon.

Three photos, U.S. Army

Repairing the Ravages of War

On April 1, 1945, the 737th and 749th Railway Operating Battalions arrived on Luzon to take over operation and restoration of 234 miles of Manila Railroad mainline from San Fernando (La Union) to Calamba, an important junction thirty-five miles south of Manila. The remainder of the 712-mile railway was operated by civilians. The 790th took over operation of the Tarlac–San Jose branch line, while the 5202 Army Engineers continued rebuilding bridges almost as soon as they were taken from the Japanese. The 131st, 132nd, and 133rd Railway Workshops Mobile came at the end of March and the 753rd Railway Shop Battalion came from Italy after V-J Day in September, to take over the main shops at Caloocan, in the Manila suburbs. An augmented Railway Grand Division, designated the 775th, was quickly established to command the operation of the Luzon Military Railway, as the mainline was called. A wrecking train operated by "B" Company of the 749th (*left*) at Caloocan was powered by a 42-inch gauge Army 2-8-2, one of 53 locomotives and 990 cars brought in from the United States. As in Burma, jeeps (*lower left*) made good emergency motive power. This one was pulling three carloads of gasoline to the front. Prefabricated boxcars, shipped directly from the United States, were assembled at Caloocan Shops (*below*) by men of the 131st Railway Workshop Mobile on May 17, 1945. By October, 1945, the MRS in the Philippines totaled 126 officers, 3,074 enlisted men, and over 6,000 civilians. In addition, the 770th ROB passed through at that time, en route from Alaska to occupation duty in Korea. The Manila Railroad was returned to its board of directors on January 1, 1946, and the Philippines granted independence by the United States on July 4 of that year.

Three photos, U.S. Army

Restoring the Railways of China

As the Japanese advance in China was stopped, then reversed, and their airpower destroyed, rebuilding of the ravaged Chinese railway network proceeded rapidly. Although no MRS units were sent to China, American Army Engineers performed much of the bridge, structures, right-of-way, and mechanical repair work, usually in an advisory or supervisory capacity. Bridge building progressed rapidly on the Kwangsi-Kweichow Railroad in southeastern China. At a highway underpass three miles north of Nantan (*above*) in Kwangsi Province, U.S. Army Engineers ran a preliminary survey while other Americans assisted Chinese rail officials (*left*) on the timber arch bridge at kilo 291 on the K-K Railroad on April 14, 1945. Another U.S. Engineer went to work on the plumbing of a shrapnel-riddled locomotive (*upper right*) "somewhere in the China, Burma, India theater," according to the noncommital wartime Signal Corps photo caption. While over 700,000 coolies worked to carve out the B-29 bases in China, thousands more backed their efforts on the railway lines that brought construction materials to the base complexes. China's greatest asset, manpower, did all of the work normally performed by heavy machinery in the West, such as coaling locomotives (*right*) at the Shiao Tsing Kai engine terminal.

Four photos, U.S. Army

Air Raids Close to Home

Two of the oldest of Japan's "overseas provinces," Formosa and Korea, came under increasing aerial attack as the Allies advanced on the island empire from three sides. Caught by a plane of the 39th Bomb Group, the locomotive of a Japanese train on the west coast of Formosa (*left*) was uncoupled by a direct hit on the cab and raced down the track after the bomber. The force of the explosion blew open the smokebox door of the engine, and the bodies of the crewmen lay on either side of the tracks, directly in front of the tender at the top of the picture. Philippine-based B-25's dropped parafrag bombs on Chickunan yards (*right*), also on Formosa. So low was the plane that the chutes of the two bombs in the foreground had barely opened when they hit, and a third bomb was about to slam into the boxcar at left. Adding insult to injury, the Americans dropped hundreds of propaganda leaflets, which were fluttering down among the bomb bursts on the station platforms. On July 4, 1945, a train pulled into Ri Ri, Korea (*above*) and was hit by U.S. Navy fighters. Seconds later, the locomotive boiler exploded.

Three photos, Indian Ministry of Defence

The Last Moments of Empire

Although the Japanese government capitulated to the Allied demand of unconditional surrender on August 15, 1945, and the formal signing was made on September 2, it took weeks longer for the word to reach isolated units of the Japanese forces, and additional time to arrange for the delicate business of all cessation of hostilities and disarmament of the vanquished troops. During September, 1945, however, virtually all of the three million survivors of the Japanese armed forces gave up. At Mokpalin, on the Sittang River in Burma, fully armed troops of the Japanese 53rd Infantry Division were loaded on flatcars (*above*) by Gurkha troops of the 17th Indian Division to be shipped to a convenient depot for disarmament. This location was especially poignant to the 17th Division, for it was at Mokpalin in 1942 that remnants of that unit surrendered to the seemingly omnipotent Japanese. At this time, troops of the Japanese expeditionary force in Bangkok, Thailand (*below*) were lined up by their officers to turn over their weapons and entrain for internment camps. On September 13 a fully armed and equipped Japanese infantry unit awaited transportation (*upper right*) at the station in Canton, China. Only six days after the final surrender, the U.S. 7th Division was establishing the occupation of South Korea. Radio operator Corporal Jack Adkins (*right*) went about his business while three Japanese officers, still carrying their map pouches and samurai swords, looked on in amusement, in front of the railway depot in Kyongsong. Barely a month earlier, the bespectacled corporal would have been in a tight spot here, indeed!

Two photos, USAF

B-29's Finish the Job

For over a year, from the spring of 1944 until August, 1945, the gigantic Boeing Superfortresses pounded the Japanese home islands, destroying the industries and railway centers that supplied the armed forces. The deadliest payloads carried by the B-29's were not the atomic bombs that obliterated Hiroshima and Nagasaki and, ultimately, Japan's will to resist, but were instead the firebombs that burned out the hearts of sixty-nine cities. On May 29, 1945, five hundred B-29's dropped tens of thousands of incendiaries (*left*) on Yokohama. On July 16 the big bombers (*above*) visited an undisclosed target. The A-bombs, terrible as they were, added only 3 per cent to the total B-29 destruction, and in one night Superfort incendiaries killed more people in Tokyo than the combined casualty toll of both the nuclear-bombed cities.

A Peaceful Occupation

The ultimate victory of strategic bombing during the Second World War was the fact that, unlike Europe, the last great battles of the Pacific were not fought in the taking of a major belligerent's homeland. Without the devastating B-29 raids that killed hundreds of thousands of human beings in the raging fire storms, a land invasion of Japan would have been necessary, with a probable death toll in excess of two million in the densely populated islands. On Victory over Japan (V-J) Day, September 2, 1945, the formal surrender was signed on board the battleship U.S.S. *Missouri* anchored in Tokyo Bay. Japan was immediately invaded by a horde of photographers and a sizable army of occupation. On that September 2 Stanley

Troutman, a photographer for Acme, recorded the devastation at the main railroad station (*above*) in Tokyo. A greater tragedy perhaps than the loss of the building was the fact that all of the wartime photographs of the Japanese National Railways were stored there when the B-29's hit. What little remained elsewhere was destroyed by frightened officials as the occupation army approached. On September 20 U.S. troops explored the wrecked terminal (*lower left*) at Yokohama. A Marine Corps Protestant chaplain, George W. Wickersham (*lower right*) still wore a pistol in a shoulder holster as he inspected a diminutive locomotive that had been camouflaged preparatory to the invasion that never came.

Two photos, UPI   *Railroad Magazine*

Repatriation and Reconstruction

In Europe World War II ended when German forces, in control of small portions of Germany, Czechoslovakia, Austria, and Italy, as well as part of Holland and all of Denmark and Norway, surrendered unconditionally to the Allies on May 7, 1945. The following day—May 8—was declared Victory in Europe (V-E) Day. The railroads of Europe lay in ruin and the mainlines that had been returned to service were in need of massive permanent rebuilding —a job that was to take almost a decade to complete, even under priority conditions and financed by the seemingly boundless generosity of the United States through the Marshall Plan. This aid, meted out impartially to former enemy and ally alike, greatly assisted the railways of Italy and Germany, as well as those of the former captive nations. Additionally, the United States was never paid much of the money owed it for Lend-Lease, including the 1,900 steam and fifty diesel locomotives that were sent to the Soviet Union, not to mention thousands of cars.

In Germany millions of displaced persons and prisoners of war were processed and returned by rail to their homelands or to start new lives in other continents. Other things were returned too, including millions of dollars' worth of stolen art treasures that were aboard Göring's private train when it was captured. Russian railway engineers relaid the main lines to Berlin in five-foot gauge, and Stalin arrived at the Potsdam Conference in July, 1945 riding behind a red-starred 0-10-0 steam locomotive.

The exact extent of military railway projects carried out during the war may never be known, but some of the statistics pertaining to just the United States Army effort are overwhelming: enough track laid to construct a double-track line from New York to Tokyo; over six hundred trestles erected, consuming more than thirty million man-hours in the Corps of Engineers alone. These figures do not even include the work of the Railway Battalions, which were directly responsible for establishing and maintaining railways in eighteen countries.

The Irony of War

The last mission performed by the 2nd Company, 1st Regiment, of an *Eisenbahnpioniere* division was to demolish a railway bridge as they retreated past Endersbach. A few hours later the unit was captured by American forces, who marched them right back to the wrecked bridge and set them to work rebuilding the span, under the direction of Company "A," 370th U.S. Army Engineer Battalion. On July 6, 1945, the German company commander, flanked by the commander and the first sergeant of the American unit, rode the first locomotive —a German 44 Class 2-10-0 (*left*)—across the completed bridge. The German officer's precise thoughts on this ironic occasion are not revealed by the laconic expression on his face.

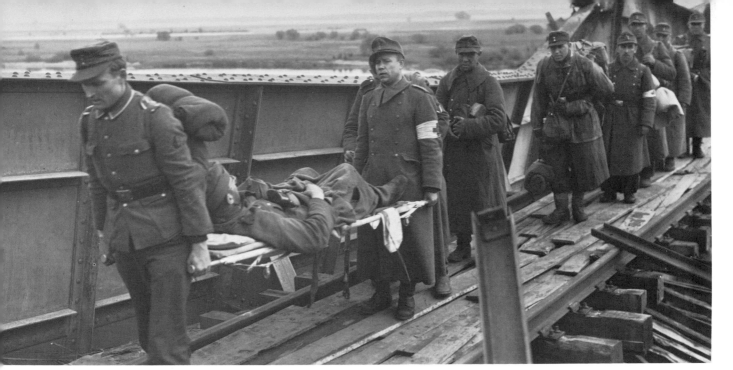

Faces of Defeat and Liberation

Fleeing the advance of the avenging Red Army, German troops, some wounded (*upper left*) crossed the wrecked railroad bridge over the Elbe River at Tangermunde to surrender to the U.S. Ninth Army just four days before the end of the war in Europe. a few weeks earlier, hundreds of German POW's (*center left*) waited in the railroad yard in Naumberg for trains to carry them to internment in France. On May 13, during the first week of peace, German soldiers (*lower left*) paused in their work of restoring the railway station in Bolzano, Italy, as a train discharged its passengers. At Weimar, two months after liberation, Polish DP's, obviously well recovered from the vicissitudes of the previous six years, received their bread ration (*above*), supplied by the United Nations Relief and Rehabilitation Administration, before boarding cars that were to take them to Bavaria. Preferring to remain in Germany rather than return to their homeland which had been overrun by Communist armies, thousands of Poles never went home. The UNRRA carried on many relief projects after the war, from feeding DP's to supplying new American-built steam locomotives to China. Frequently DP's could be as unruly and troublesome on trains as SS prisoners, creating a nuisance for Allied railway troops, who tried to treat the civilians as agreeably as possible. When an overloaded train of French DP's stalled on a hill, the U.S. Army crew decided to wait for another locomotive to assist. The angry Frenchmen, anxious to get home, would not wait, and to a man they disembarked and pushed the train up over the hill!

The Inadvertent American Atrocity

It was a well-known fact that entire populations within the boundaries of the Soviet Union had initially welcomed the German invasion in 1941 as a great liberation. Many peoples had suffered execrable atrocities under the domination of the ruthless Moscow government, including the murders of millions of Ukranians. It should have come as no wonder to the Western Allies that thousands of these wretched human beings would welcome the chance to take up arms against their Communist oppressors and that even when "liberation" at the hands of Nazi Germany proved to be a phantasy, the burning hatred felt toward the Moscow government would remain a consuming passion. A lesser-known accord among those "Big Three" meetings of the leaders of the United States, Britain, and Russia was that all citizens of the three powers held by Nazi Germany would be returned to their country of origin. Except for a handful of traitors and capital offenders, the edict

Two photos, U.S. Army

had little effect on American or British citizens, but to millions of Russians it was, literally, a death sentence. Even ordinary Soviet Army soldiers who had fought loyally for Moscow were in mortal danger, for it was a major offense to be captured by the enemy. These Russians were well aware of their impending doom, for hundreds of Americans heard their pleas and the intentions of the Russians, but were powerless to act. If their urgent messages ever reached Washington, they were purposely kept from Harry S. Truman, who had just become President after the death, a month before the final Nazi collapse, of Franklin D. Roosevelt. Among the incidents reported was the case of an American air controller (who was a railroader in civilian life) in charge of flying thousands of Ukrainians to Poland, where they were turned over to Soviet authorities. A Russian liaison officer, puzzled at the good treatment of the "liberated slave laborers" by the Americans, explained that they would all be "eliminated" upon their return to Russia! After all, Stalin could not accept millions of people who had seen the West and been exposed to free thought—as far as Communism was concerned—under the Nazis. Unlike the happy faces of freed prisoners who were citizens of the democracies, "liberated" Russians (*above*), on the start of the journey back by train, appear very morose. Ukrainians, who tried to commit suicide rather than go back home, were herded into cages (*left*) in boxcars, under the watch of armed American MP's. Thousands succeeded in taking their own lives, several hundred having jumped off of just one train crossing over a deep canyon in Poland. All of the gruesome details of this probably unintentional atrocity committed by the highest level of the American government are contained in a thick folder, File Card No. 383.7-14.4, "Forcible Repatriation of Displaced Soviet Citizens", of the Army Historical Records Branch in Alexandria, Virginia. In spite of a law passed by Congress and signed by President Lyndon B. Johnson in 1967 that releases all such information to the public, the Army, on secret orders, refuses to release the documents. Lawsuits under the 1967 law are pending.

Clearing the Rubble

The wreckage of the Potsdamer railway terminal in Berlin (*above*), with train shed collapsed on the tracks and gutted buildings all around, was typical of the calamity visited upon the German capital by the heavy bombers of the United States and England. Photographs such as this were made by Army Air Force photographers who, having no further combat operations to record, traveled throughout Germany to capture on film the results of the strategic bombing campaign. The detractors of the bombing effort may have a point —that bombing alone did not bring down the Third Reich—but to the Allied railway men who were charged with getting the trains running again, the air raids were a decisive factor. If one considers the fact that most of the *Luftwaffe*, thousands of soldiers in antiaircraft units, thousands of guns, and millions of shells, as well as hundreds of thousands of workers who were involved in clearing bomb damage, were tied up by the air war, the disruption it caused becomes even more evident. Men of Company "B," 265th Engineer Battalion, U.S. Army (*below*), utilized narrow-gauge locomotives and temporary track to clear rubble in Linz, Germany, just across the Rhine from Remagen on June 22, 1945.

UPI

USAF from Southern Railway

The Death of Roosevelt

When Franklin D. Roosevelt, President of the United States until the last month of the war, died in Hot Springs, Georgia, on April 12, 1945, his body was returned to Washington by train. Near Clemson, South Carolina, on the Charlotte Division of the Southern Railway, the funeral train (*below*) was double-headed by two of that road's beautiful, renowned green and gold PS-4 Pacifics. The second locomotive of the tandem was No. 1401, now on display in the Smithsonian Institution in Washington. Upon the arrival of Roosevelt's remains at the capital, the flag-bedecked coffin was placed on a wooden-wheeled caisson (*left*) and drawn by seven white horses to the White House for the last rites on April 15. Former Vice President Harry S. Truman was President, to see the nation through the conclusion of the war and the shaky peace, studded with violent outbursts, which followed. So ill-prepared had the late President left Truman that the new Chief Executive was not even aware of the atomic bombs then under construction, which he was to order dropped on Japan less than four months later! Undoubtedly he also knew nothing of the millions of doomed Russians who even then were being readied for their last long train rides—to firing squads or the slower death of Siberian concentration camps.

Collection of James A. Corwin

Liberation Engines for France

With only three thousand operable steam locomotives—less than one-fifth of the prewar total—left at the time of liberation, the French National Railways needed a massive infusion of motive power to return to the credo by which it operated: "To serve." Although hundreds of French engines were recovered from Germany and hundreds more of the unserviceable ones were being returned to active status at the rate of forty a day in the SNCF shops by 1946, they were, like the original survivors in France, worn from years of wartime abuse. The French had found that the reliable GI 2-8-0's were too much of a military compromise to form the backbone of their postwar locomotive roster, so they turned to the great locomotive builders of North America in March, 1945, to construct a "Liberation class" locomotive in great numbers and in a great hurry. The three biggest United States locomotive builders—Baldwin, American, and Lima—and the two largest Canadian firms—Montreal and Canadian—turned out 1,340 of the Class 141R 2-8-2 type dual-service engines, beginning in July, 1945. All but seventeen of them, which went down in the North Atlantic, put in long years of service and were a major factor in getting the French economy back in shape. A quarter-century after they were built, hundreds of the 141R's were still in service on the SNCF, but were slated for eventual replacement by diesel power or electrification. Although the builders of North America were still turning out thousands of steam locomotives annually for domestic use and export at the end of the war, by 1949 all production had ceased and a scant decade later the railroads of the United States had sent the forty thousand steam locomotives that had carried the freight of victory, plus hundreds built in the late 1940's, to the scrap yards. The postwar "baby boom" of the North American locomotive industry lived longer in the form of Liberation 141R's shown at Lima (*above*) and on the stationary test plant at American (*below*) than it did on its own continent.

National Archives

The Victors Return Home

The railway lines to Berlin and Tokyo had been long ones, hard fought and rebuilt through sheer stamina and unconquerable human spirit. With the work of war behind them, fifty million soldiers of a score of nations prepared to return home. For virtually all of them—vanquished and victor—a good part of that journey would be by rail. Some rode in cattle cars, others in double bedrooms on the *Twentieth Century Limited*, but they were all homeward bound, their warring days over. That is what really mattered. Ironically, it was after the war, in December, 1945, that crisis finally overtook the great American domestic railroad system. The combination of the first Christmas in four years with relaxed civilian travel restrictions, plus the discharge of over one million servicemen that

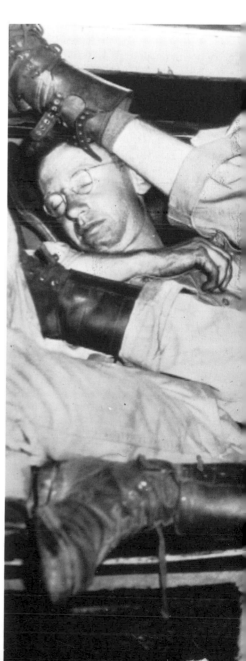

month and millions more on furlough, created a passenger-car demand that far outweighed the supply —and Americans just do not travel in boxcars! The result saw weary veterans having to spend days at a stretch in coaches (*below*) as their first experience after returning from the battlefronts. Still, there never was a total breakdown in service, just delays. Military railroaders like James R. Boerckel of the 733rd Railway Operating Battalion, along with his beer-guzzling buddies, celebrated their departure from Germany (*right*) and came home to show the civilians how to run a railroad. Many Russians experienced delays in getting home as well, such as the senior artillery lieutenant (*left*) seen sitting on his belongings as he awaited a departing train at a bombed-out depot in destroyed, divided, occupied Berlin.

Railroad Magazine

Collection of James R. Boerckel

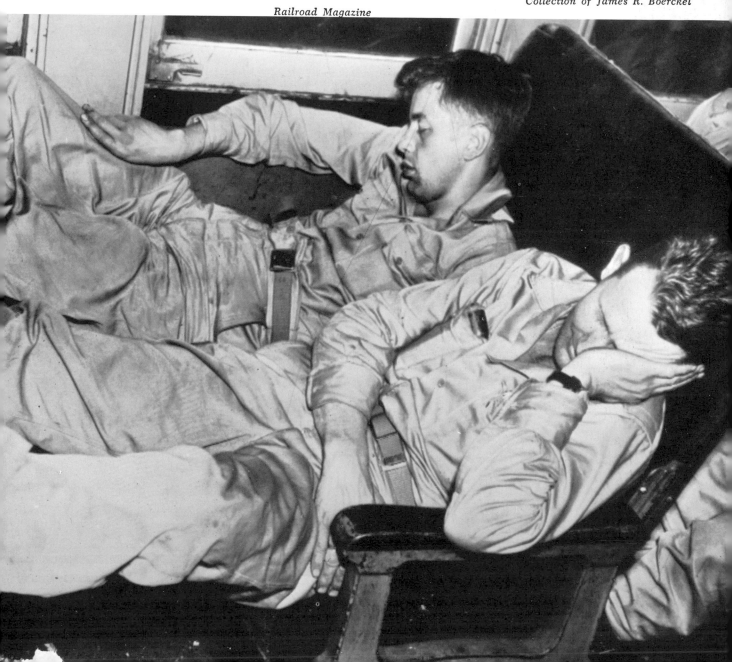

MILITARY RAILWAY UNITS, UNITED STATES ARMY

Railway Grand Divisions

Unit	Sponsor	Date of Activation
701st	New York Central Railroad	January 11, 1943
702nd	Union Pacific Railroad	October 15, 1942
703rd	Atlantic Coast Line Railroad	August 1, 1942
704th	Great Northern Railway	November 30, 1942
705th	Southern Pacific Lines	May 19, 1943
706th	Pennsylvania Railroad	October 6, 1943
707th	Southern Railway	June 10, 1943
708th	Baltimore & Ohio Railroad	April 6, 1943
709th	Association of American Railroads	March 15, 1944
710th	Atchison, Topeka & Santa Fe Railway	December 14, 1943
774th	(No sponsorship: Organized in Italy)	1944

Unit	Sponsor	Date of Activation
745th	Chicago, Burlington & Quincy	May 19, 1943
746th	Missouri-Kansas-Texas Railroad	May 4, 1944
747th	Atchison, Topeka & Santa Fe	never activated
748th	Texas & Pacific Railway	May 12, 1943
749th	New York, New Haven & Hartford Railroad	February 23, 1944
750th	St. Louis–San Francisco Railway	March 21, 1944
751st	Denver & Rio Grande Western	never activated
752nd	Boston & Maine Railroad	May 4, 1944
759th	Missouri Pacific Railroad	September 1, 1942
770th	no sponsorship	August 9, 1942
790th	no sponsorship	July 8, 1943
761st Railway Transportation Company *		July 22, 1942

Railway Operating Battalions

Unit	Sponsor	Date of Activation
711th	Training Battalion—not sponsored	May 1, 1941
712th	Central Railroad of New Jersey	October 25, 1942
713th	Atchison, Topeka & Santa Fe	April 15, 1942
714th	Chicago, St. Paul, Minneapolis & Omaha	October 31, 1942
715th	Illinois Central Railroad	October 31, 1942
716th	Southern Pacific Lines	December 21, 1943
717th	Pennsylvania Railroad	December 1, 1943
718th	Cleveland, Cincinnati, Chicago & St. Louis	December 14, 1943
719th	Texas & New Orleans Railroad	September 1, 1943
720th	Chicago & Northwestern	August 26, 1943
721st	New York Central Railroad	April 14, 1943
722nd	Seaboard Air Line Railroad	December 14, 1943
723rd	Union Pacific Railroad	December 28, 1943
724th	Pennsylvania Railroad	December 28, 1943
725th	Chicago, Rock Island & Pacific	February 17, 1944
726th	Wabash Railroad	June 26, 1943
727th	Southern Railway	March 15, 1942
728th	Louisville & Nashville Railroad	January 11, 1943
729th	New York, New Haven & Hartford Railroad	January 11, 1943
730th	Pennsylvania Railroad	May 15, 1942
731st	Union Pacific Railroad	never activated
732nd	Great Northern Railway	January 12, 1944
733rd	Central of Georgia Railway	November 23, 1943
734th	Texas & New Orleans Railroad	February 23, 1944
735th	Association of American Railroads	February 10, 1944
736th	New York Central Railroad	never activated
737th	New York Central Railroad	September 30, 1944
738th	Chicago Great Western Railway	never activated
739th	Lehigh Valley Railroad	never activated
740th	Chesapeake & Ohio Railway	December 14, 1943
741st	Gulf, Mobile & Ohio Railroad	January 12, 1944
742nd	Pennsylvania Railroad	never activated
743rd	Illinois Central Railroad	January 12, 1944
744th	Chicago, Milwaukee, St. Paul & Pacific	December 21, 1943

Railway Shop Battalions

Unit	Sponsor	Date of Activation
753rd †	Cleveland, Cincinnati, Chicago & St. Louis	April 15, 1942
754th †	Southern Pacific Lines	October 15, 1942
755th †	Norfolk & Western Railway	November 30, 1943
756th †	Pennsylvania Railroad	January 11, 1943
757th †	Chicago, Milwaukee, St. Paul & Pacific	June 10, 1943
758th †	Atchison, Topeka & Santa Fe	April 6, 1943
760th ‡	no sponsorship	June 15, 1942
762nd ‡	no sponsorship	October 15, 1942
763rd †	Delaware, Lackawanna & Western	July 27, 1943
	Lehigh Valley Railroad	
764th †	Boston & Maine Railroad	October 25, 1943
765th †	Erie Railroad	May 1, 1944
766th †	Association of American Railroads	July 17, 1944

* The 761st RTC was the advance party in England. Later it performed switching duties in large terminals; it was never elevated to battalion status.
† Railway Shop Battalion (Steam).
‡ Railway Shop Battalion (Diesel). There was no sponsorship because of lack of experience with diesels. Personnel were specialists from many fields of internal combustion power.

Most of the above units were deactivated as soon as their sectors could be returned to civilian operation after cessation of hostilities, the last being in April, 1946. The 712th, 714th, 724th, and 765th were recalled for duty in the Korean War (1950–1953). By 1969 the 714th, on reduced status, was the only active railway unit left in the armed forces of the United States; it was stationed at Fort Eustis, Virginia.

Recommended Reading

Railways in Wartime, by E. F. Carter; London: Frederick Muller, Ltd., 1964. *Railroading in Eighteen Countries*, by Major General Carl R. Gray, Jr.; New York: Charles Scribner's Sons, 1955. *Rail Transport and the Winning of Wars*, by General James A. Van Fleet; Washington, D.C.: Association of American Railroads, 1956. *Facts about British Railways in Wartime*, by The British Railways Press Office; London: 1943. *Survey of International Affairs, 1939–1946, Hitler's Europe*, edited by Arnold and Veronica M. Toynbee; London: Oxford University Press, 1954. *U.S. Army in World War II, The Technical Services, The Transportation Corps*, by Chester Wardlow; Washington, D.C.: Office of the Chief of Military History, United States Army, 1951.

Southern Railway

Leaders of the 727th

MRS Director General Colonel (later Major General) Carl R. Gray, Jr., fifth from left; Lieutenant Colonel Fred Okie, commander of the Southern Railway–sponsored 727th Railway Operating Battalion, third from left; and Southern Director-General Hungerford (in civilian clothes) with Colonel Okie's staff at Fort Northeastern during the training of the 727th.

Index

Showing the pages in which illustrations appear in boldface numerals.

Freight Destined for Hiroshima and Nagasaki

The incredibly beautiful, though dying, Rio Grande Southern Railroad, a desolate and legendary narrow gauge which was in its last years of operation in southwestern Colorado during World War II, experienced a sudden surge of freight business at the time. Local miners, when they could get close enough to view the trainloads of ore carried by the RGS behind leased Denver & Rio Grande Western locomotives such as No. 464 (*below*), were amazed that anybody could have any interest in the worthless-looking stuff. It was only after the dawn of the Atomic Age over the Japanese cities of Hiroshima and Nagasaki which ended the war, that it was learned that rich uranium ore had been the mysterious freight which prompted a final season of bonanza for the fading Colorado narrow gauge.

Lucius Beebe photo from Charles Clegg

Postscript: The Military Railway Situation Twenty-five Years Later

It is perhaps understandable that a government which has allowed the civilian railways—lifeblood of its commerce and vehicle of its own defense—to deteriorate to the extent of the American railroad system would allow the bitterly learned lessons of military history to be forgotten as well. By the peak of another conflict—the Vietnam, or Indochina, war—nearly a quarter-century after World War II, the U.S. Army carried only one Railway Battalion on its rolls. Indeed, that unit, the 714th, stationed at Fort Eustis, Virginia, had been allowed to fall way under strength and was referred to as a Transportation Battalion. There was talk of deactivation of the 714th, even as the last four of its steam locomotives were phased out of service.

Although there are a few railway units in inactive reserve status and although there are veterans of the World War II Military Railway Service available to form a cadre should the need for a new MRS arise, the railway defenses of the United States have been let down to a dangerous extent. This is due in part to the tactics of Vietnam—a minor campaign by World War II standards—which is essentially a guerrilla-war situation where the few rail lines were made inoperative early in the conflict and where, because of the minor distances involved, supply of troops in the field can be handled by other means of transport. Should a major war break out, the Vietnam logistics would not be adequate for one week. Better lessons in rail-

way logistics since World War II were learned by the United States in Korea and later, during the Cuban Missile Crisis of 1962, when the railroads of the U.S. interior, *on six hours' notice,* moved an entire invasion force into Florida, without disrupting the regular operations of the lines involved. More recently, the Sino-Soviet dispute has involved the movement of entire armies by rail. The major Communist powers have not forgotten the importance of railways in strategic planning!

The fact is that in a future major conflict aircraft and trucks could never supply the forces in the field over great distances; the *Red Ball Express* in Europe and the inherent limitations of aviation, including the C-5A and future "jumbo" jets, have proved this cardinal rule of logistics time and again. As a final warning to be considered, the incredible blunder of destroying all of the coal-burning steam locomotives may someday leave entire combat areas with an intact rail system nevertheless rendered useless by the simple expedient of sabotaging a few electric-power substations or imposing a blockade to halt the flow of oil for diesel fuel. The World War II examples of steam-locomotive flexibility and other lessons referred to in this volume have all been forgotten by the strategists of NATO. They can only hope that their potential adversaries have forgotten as well. Indications are that they have not.

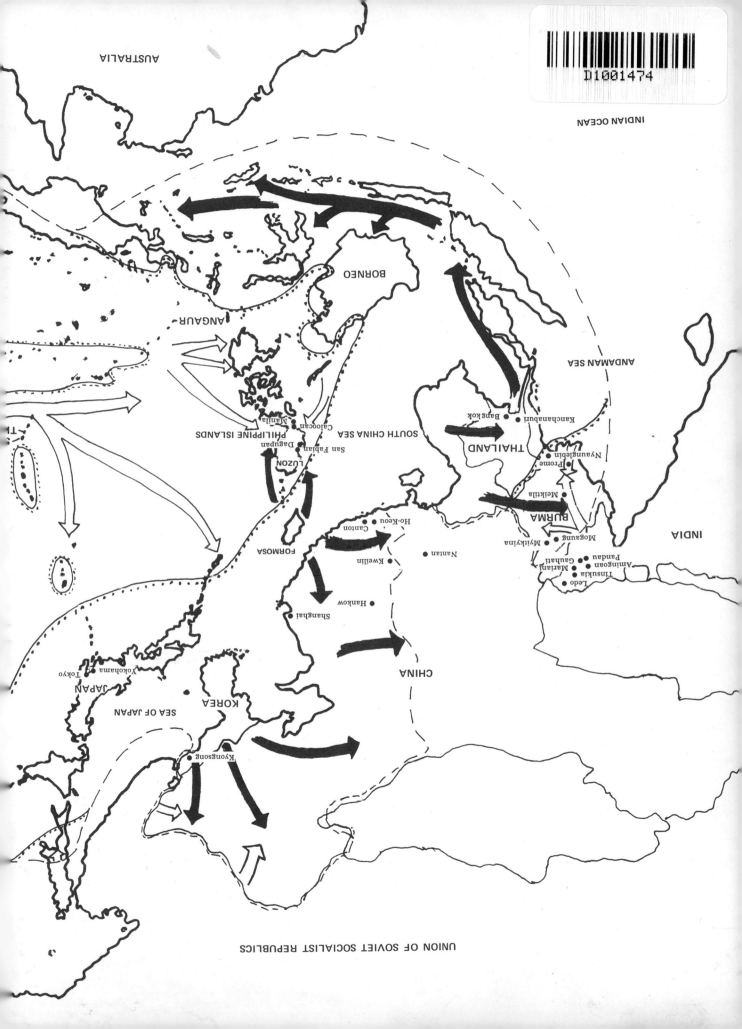